W9-CUG-116

The Finest Rooms

*by America's
Great Decorators*

The Finest Rooms

by America's Great Decorators

INTRODUCTION BY RUSSELL LYNES

EDITED BY KATHARINE TWEED

Bramhall House · New York

PHOTOGRAPHIC ACKNOWLEDGMENTS

The design of the book, space requirements, and the undesirability of credit repetition demanded that acknowledgments to photographs be given on a separate page instead of under the pictures themselves, except for the historical pictures used in the Introduction. The pages on which the work of each contributing photographer appears are listed below after his name.

Louis H. Frohman: pages 33-39, 58, 66-68, 76 (top), 108-109, 110 (top), 111, 115, 152, 153.
Henry S. Fullerton 3rd: pages 70, 75, 78, 81, 83, 86-88, 90-94, 102-106, 110 (bottom), 119-21, 128, 141, 144-46, 149-51, 154, 155.
Harold Haliday Costain: pages 47-50, 55-57, 136.
André Kertesz: pages 20, 21, 56 (bottom), 99-101, 126, 130, 131, 134.
Fred Lyon: pages 159-62, 165, 166.
Ernst Beadle: page 163 (courtesy *Ladies' Home Journal*).
B. Boucher: pages 132, 133.

Haanel Cassidy: pages 58, 63, 69.
David Hirsch: page 114.
Samuel H. Gottscho: pages 82, 142, 148.
Wendy Hilty: page 42.
Kern Studio: page 122.
Tom Leonard: pages 64, 84, 85.
Wayne Miller: pages 156, 164, 165.
Alfredo de Molli: page 116.
Hans Namuth: pages 112, 113.
Emelie Nicholson: page 72.
Hans van Nes: page 77.

Library of Congress catalog card number: 64-20859

This edition published by Bramhall House
a division of Clarkson N. Potter, Inc.,
by arrangement with the Viking Press, Inc.
b c d e f g h

Printed in the U.S.A.

Book designed by Bryan Holme

Contents

This book is dedicated to the late Harold Guinzburg, whose idea it originally was.

Those who knew him have devoted extra care and time in its preparation, in the hope that the book would have pleased him.

EDITOR'S ACKNOWLEDGMENTS

In the making of this book, which took over three years to complete, a great many people have contributed their help, advice, enthusiasm, and patience, without so much as a thought of recognition or reward. Without them, however, the book could have been neither planned, organized, nor completed.

My sincere thanks, therefore to Miss Sylvia Wilson of Smyth, Urquhart and Marckwald; Miss Eleanore Detwiler of McMillen, Inc.; Miss Ruth Schwich of Baldwin and Martin. Thanks also, of a personal kind, to Marian Hall, whose wise and humorous advice helped steer us through, and around, many unexpected crises; and to all the decorators represented on these pages and their assistants and associates who have contributed so much time and patience in producing the texts and helping to arrange for the necessary photographs to be taken. Special acknowledgment is due also to Emily Davie, who worked so hard in the planning stages of the book, and to the staff of The Viking Press for their wonderful cooperation from beginning to end.

The majority of the photographs shown on the following pages were taken especially for this book by arrangement with Louis H. Frohman and Henry S. Fullerton 3rd. Their enthusiastic interest, meticulous care, and uncompromising use of their technical skills has been most appreciated.

Acknowledgment is also made to the other excellent photographers for the photographs noted on page 4. A particular word of thanks goes to Condé Nast for permitting the reproduction of some of the rooms originally photographed for *Vogue* and *House & Garden*.

The portraits of the decorators on the back jacket were all (with the exception of the one of Rose Cumming) generously donated by the photographer, Wilbur Pippin.

Above all my thanks, and those of the publishers, decorators, and photographers, go to the owners of the rooms illustrated, for sharing with us the conviction that this book would be a valuable contribution to the literature on American taste (and decoration), and for allowing us, often at considerable inconvenience to themselves, to photograph, in their houses and apartments, these "finest rooms."

—KATHARINE TWEED

Enter
the Decorator

AN INTRODUCTION

$\mathcal{J}$F YOU WILL READ THE SHORT, REVEALING ARTICLES OF FAITH BY THE DECORATORS WHOSE rooms embellish this book, you will discover, as I have, something of the nature of a mysterious profession.

Interior decoration, as professions go, is quite a new one, scarcely older than our century. Like those of the architect and the landscapist and the planner, the decorator's profession is concerned with the creation of environment, but, while it is an accepted part of the designer's function to imprint his special style upon his work, it is the function of the decorator to vanish. A home (as distinct from the structure of a house) is meant to reflect the personality of its inhabitants—a precept that you will find stated in various ways in the text and pictures of this book. The room is most successful as an example of the decorator's art that seems least contrived by its contriver, that most amiably and handsomely reflects the image of its owner and that, at the same time, seems to have happened spontaneously. Decorating is an exercise in taste, a word and a concept that defies definition. It is often an exercise in compromise, a word that does not exist at all in some modern languages. It is also an exercise in alchemy, a long discredited medieval science of making precious objects out of base ones. Decorating is, as I have suggested, a mysterious profession.

A century ago there was no such thing as an interior decorator in America, though that is not to say that there was not a great deal of interest in the decorating of houses or that a great deal of time and money and loving care was not expended on the interiors in which our great- and great-great-grandparents lived. There were furniture designers, of course, designers of fabrics and carpets, and there were upholsterers. It was the upholsterer's shop that came closest to fulfilling the function of the decorator. He supplied advice as well as fabrics and furniture, draperies with lambrequins, ottomans, and tasseled table covers. Upholsterers were the delight of women and

Parlor in a New York House. Drawing from *Ballou's Pictorial*, 1854.

the despair of their husbands, who looked upon them as evokers of women's most extravagant tendencies and as persons hell-bent on making man's life miserable by their insistence on the sacrifice of comfort to the rigorous demands of fashion.

The profession of interior decorator did not arise spontaneously to meet a sudden need. It emerged toward the end of the last century at a time when America was about to be smothered under a drift of bric-à-brac, plush, needlepoint spaniels, Brussels carpets, dos-à-dos, and potted palms. It was not enough that there was a whatnot in the corner of the parlor filled with nostalgic mementos. Mansions were like the insides of little boys' pockets, filled with the grown-up equivalents of bits of string and rusty nails and marbles and pretty pebbles and baseball cards and arrowheads. Paintings of cows in misty landscapes, moon-eyed maidens, and medieval castles against angry skies hung on flock-covered walls in tiers one above the other from wainscoting to ceiling. Rosewood chairs of uncompromisingly moral posture stood rigidly about tables on which sat parlor books filled with sentimental narratives in verse, with little homilies for maidens, and hand-tinted pictures to accompany the vocabulary of the language of the flowers. Taste was everywhere —on pincushions, on washstands and shaving stands, on the spindled cornices of parlor organs, the mantels draped with satin and ball fringe, the plate rails in the dining room crowned with Delft and beer steins and ornamental tiles. America was in need of a rummage sale.

The clutter had accumulated for about seventy years before the decorators started to clear it out, and it had been accumulated in the name of taste—indeed, to start with, in the name of classical taste.

Let me explain. To do so I must take a step backward.

There was a distinct shift in taste in America in the late 1820s and early 1830s with the arrival of what has been called the First Age of the Common Man. The election of Andrew Jackson to the presidency marked the end of the political sway of the old aristocracy, which had been dominated by the landed gentry of the South and by such families as the Adamses of the North. There was a new wave of republicanism and egalitarianism which coincided with a new era in manufacture of household furnishings of all sorts. Not only was there tremendous optimism about the future of the nation and about the opportunities for any man with wit and energy to succeed and take his place as a leader in the community, but there was a wave of middle-class gentility. This gentility expressed itself partly with a new concern about manners (there came a flood of books of etiquette) and also with the exercise of taste about one's surroundings. The first new fad was for the classical and more specifically for the Greek Revival.

It is difficult for us to realize today that the Greek Revival house with its free-standing porticoes of columns or with its pilasters, its pediments, and tall narrow windows was as common in America in the forties of the last century as the ranch house is today. But everyone who could afford to build or to remodel wanted the Greek touches that bespoke on the one hand the republican's affinity with ancient republics and on the other the fight of a nation for its inde-

Shelley Smith.

Parlor floor of the Old Merchant's House, New York, 1830.

"Andalusia," Residence of Nicholas Biddle near Philadelphia. Designed by Nicholas Biddle and T. U. Walter, 1833.

pendence. The interior of the Greek Revival house (it came in all sizes from the massive Andalusia built by the banker Nicholas Biddle near Philadelphia to the farmer's cottage) tended at first to be rather chaste. Scenic wallpapers were out of fashion, tinted walls in gentle tones were in. Furniture had a somewhat Empire severity, and upholstery was likely to be horsehair or somber plush. Columns were almost inevitable in the wide door that characteristically separated the front from the back parlor in city houses, and crystal chandeliers hung from molded ceilings. The mirror over the white-marble mantel was a symbol of status. Those most prized were imported French ones in gilt frames.

The fashion for Greek Revival lasted well beyond the middle of the century, though it was mostly Westerners who by then were building it. (The Mississippi was very far west in those days, and in the 1850s it took a full decade for a fashion in women's clothes, and far longer in houses, to get from Boston to St. Louis.) In the East, and especially in the Hudson Valley, a new style, introduced by the landscapist and the most influential tastemaker of his day, Andrew Jackson Downing, became the apple of the eye of those with up-to-date taste. It was the Gothic Revival with its peaked, slate roofs, turrets, and crenelations that supplanted the Greek Revival or "temple" style. Downing, who had learned his aesthetic doctrine at the feet of Ruskin and Pugin, the champions of Gothic Revival in England, declared that it was utter nonsense for Americans to live in temples—houses of the gods with brick chimneys protruding from their roofs; Gothic was far more suitable. If this nice distinction between the world of togas and that of chain mail as proper for American farmers and merchants is difficult for us to understand, the followers of Downing (and they were legion) agreed with him, and not only exteriors changed but so did interiors. Parlor chairs became little bishops' thrones; desks became altars; ladies in their crinolines looked out of leaded glass windows at lawns whose flower beds and evergreens were like punctuation marks—commas filled with cannas, brighter than fire, conical firs and spherical yews clipped like exclamation points and periods. The Gothic furniture that suited these houses, it is worth noting, was not ancient, not antique; it was newly made by such designers and manufacturers as George Platt of New York, whom Downing admired.

Fashion stepped lightly, if not very sure-footedly, from Gothic to the so-called Switz cottage

Wayne Andrews.

The drawing room at "Andalusia."

"Mr. and Mrs. Ernest Fiedler and Family." Oil painting, 1850.

with its wide, Alpine eaves and shallow-pitched roofs, to the Tuscan villa (quite unlike anything in Tuscany that I have ever seen) with its corner tower, tiles, and wide, bracketed porches, to the Mansard house (sometimes called General Grant but now usually referred to as "Charles Addams"). The typical Mansard, though it came in a great variety of shapes and sizes, tended to be symmetrical with a center tower flanked by verandas and crowned with ornamental ironwork.

Meanwhile the clutter indoors was increasing. The "lightness, elegance, and grace" of what was known in Downing's day as "the French taste" began to lose its agreeable character under the sheer weight of more and more of everything—gaudier Brussels carpets, fancier lambrequins, more preposterous arrangements of wax flowers and stuffed birds under bell glasses, more crudely designed, heavier, and clumsier furniture dangling with more fringe. The time was obviously approaching when someone was going to have to produce a gigantic broom and sweep the nation out.

If there were as yet no interior decorators to undertake this Augean endeavor, there were writers about taste by the score and architects producing books filled with plans and pictures and words of advice to the householder about what he should do to be sensible as well as tasteful. In the 1870s the most influential of the writers was an Englishman, Charles Locke Eastlake, the nephew of the president of the Royal Society, a then famous and now forgotten painter, Sir Charles Eastlake. The young Eastlake wrote a little book, illustrated with drawings of furniture and rooms and samples of wallpaper, called *Hints on Household Taste*. It landed like a plastic bomb in the American household and shattered in a resounding explosion what very nearly all right-thinking people had considered to be the doctrines of good taste.

"Suddenly the voice of the prophet Eastlake was heard crying in the wilderness," exclaimed the editors of *Harper's Bazar* [sic], "Repent ye, for the Kingdom of the Tasteful is at hand!"

Out with the curlicues, out with the fringe, out with the fancy veneers and machine-carved furbelows and fruit-carved mantels! Down with the damask draperies, the glittering chandeliers, the pargeted ceilings! But above all, down with pretense! Down with sham! Down with aesthetic quackery!

The Brooklyn Museum.

Drawing room from the Robert J. Milligan house in Saratoga Springs, 1854-1856.

And up, of course, with honesty! Up with sincerity!

Eastlake was a proponent of the handicraft movement of which William Morris was the guiding spirit and the philosopher. Honesty to Eastlake was a rather simple matter—a matter of construction and design. To put furniture together with wooden dowels was honest; to use nails or screws was dishonest. (He was not quite so sure about veneers, though he was suspicious of anything that was not solidly what it seemed to be.) As for design, he was what we would now call a doctrinaire functionalist, at least on paper. He believed that "the essential and necessary structure of an object should never be lost sight of nor concealed by secondary forms or ornament." But anyone who is familiar with the Eastlake furniture that became so popular in the late 1870s and lingered for several more decades cannot but wonder what, in the name of sincerity, he had in mind. Eastlake furniture is, in some respects, the epitome of nineteenth century obfuscation.

Eastlake's adherents were many, and they were ardent. They believed that the ultimate in decoration and decorative objects was "the quaint" and its companion, "the artistic." It was the age of "artistic" tiles ("There is much morality in a tile," one tasteful writer of the time said), of "sincere" teapots, of "picturesque" bookcases, of peacock feathers and cattails in brass pots, of Japanese prints, of the Pre-Raphaelite hairdo. It was a time when critics spoke of ugly

Gothic cottage, 1844. Residence of Henry Delemater, Rhinebeck, New York. Designed by A. J. Davis.

A Tuscan villa depicted in a Currier and Ives print of 1855.

furniture as "immoral"; it was the time when W. S. Gilbert wrote in his operetta, *Patience*:

> You can't get high aesthetic tastes,
> Like trousers, ready made....

It was also the era when Mrs. M. E. W. Sherwood, the grandmother of the playwright, Robert Sherwood, a famous hostess of her day, could write without evident self-consciousness in *Harper's Magazine*, "The soothing influence of an Eastlake bookcase on an irritated husband has never been sufficiently calculated."

There was a style of domestic architecture that delighted Americans in the eighties and nineties (and even spilled over into the first decade of this century) that was complementary to the quaint and the artistic. It was called, for rather obscure reasons, Queen Anne. It first caught the imaginations of visitors to the great world's fair of 1876, the Centennial Exhibition, in Philadelphia. The British pavilion, out of which Queen Anne grew into something quite distinct, was a sort of Tudor country house, but as it was interpreted by American architects it was characterized by long sloping roofs, second- and third-floor balconies, Jacobean chimneys, and wide verandas. The fad for the Queen Anne became every bit as universal as the Greek Revival had been, but we are so accustomed to it still that we scarcely notice it. You will find Queen Anne houses from Portland, Maine, to Portland, Oregon. You will find them in Oklahoma and Texas and Virginia. Originally they were painted in "somber hues" or sheathed with stained shingles; white was considered a "vulgar" color for the exteriors of houses—too garish, too contrasting with the colors of nature. They frequently have octagonal or round towers on a front corner; their porches, outdoor summer living rooms, have ornamental spindles. Their plans are invariably asymmetrical,

Queen Anne house. Drawing from *Modern Dwellings* by H. Hudson Holly, 1878.

and usually the entrance hall is wide, often with a fireplace and inglenook in it, and out of it climbs a staircase with a stained-glass window on its landing. Queen Anne came in all sizes, as mammoth "cottages" at summer resorts, as small houses for clerks in suburbs.

It was "Queen Anne" who had stomped her way across America, and it was under her roofs

Wayne Andrews.

"The Breakers," 1892-1895. Dining room in the Cornelius Vanderbilt residence in Newport, Rhode Island.

"Biltmore," 1895. Hallway in the residence of George Washington Vanderbilt at Asheville, North Carolina.

that the final clutter of the last century was stowed away in attics to make room for the artistic decorations of Mr. Eastlake.

Enter the interior decorator.

It wasn't as though the decorators were the first to try to do away with the accumulated "bad taste" of the century. Downing had launched the offensive in the 1840s; *Godey's Lady's Book* had fought the fight, and so had *Harper's New Monthly Magazine* and *Harper's Bazar*. So had women like Catharine Beecher and her sister, Harriet Beecher Stowe, with books on household management and decorating. So had dozens of writers of books on domestic architecture. So had Edward Bok, the great editor of the *Ladies' Home Journal* in the 1890s, with his double-page spreads showing houses in "good taste" on one side and "bad taste" on the other. Perhaps still more important, so had a woman named Candace Wheeler who, in the 1890s, published an article in the *Outlook* called "Interior Decoration as a Profession for Women." There were few professions in those days that women could practice without offending respectability. Why not let women use their "instinctive knowledge of textiles and intimate knowledge of the convenience of domestic life"?

About ten years after Miss Wheeler made her plea, Elsie de Wolfe set herself up in business as America's first woman interior decorator. Her reputation was established when the architect Stanford White persuaded a committee of ladies to engage her services to do the interior of the Colony Club on Madison Avenue between Thirty-first and Thirty-second Streets in New York. Her fortune was made when Henry C. Frick gave her the job of furnishing the second floor of his mansion at Fifth Avenue and Seventieth Street. He paid her a 10 per cent commission on every stick of furniture that she bought for him, and he bought millions of dollars worth of it. The influence of Elsie de Wolfe, who later became Lady Mendl, is everywhere in this book.

Elsie de Wolfe was an innovator, but she was not an original philosopher of design. "Suitability" was her criterion for decoration and for every piece of furniture, picture, textile, rug, or bibelot in her interiors. It was a word that she had learned from the novelist Edith Wharton, whom she thought "sharp and cold," but who had written with the architect Henry Codman a book on interiors. "The essence of taste is suitability," Mrs. Wharton had said in another book, *French*

Elsie de Wolfe in her Cozy Corner, 1896.

Dining room designed by Elsie de Wolfe for her home, 1898.

Ways and Their Meanings. "Divest the word of its prim and priggish implications, and see how it expresses the mysterious demand of the eye and mind for symmetry, harmony, and order." Mrs. Wharton found "suitability" preferable to Eastlake's word "sincerity," and so, obviously, did Miss de Wolfe. You will find the word "suitability" used frequently in this book; it is a word that lends itself to a great variety of interpretations and tastes; and while it is not very helpful for that reason, it is certainly inoffensive, polite, and pliable. It had its uses, though, in helping to clear out the clutter of nineteenth-century claptrap and to make way for a fresh kind of eclecticism in which the emphasis was on quality rather than on any consistent style.

Unfortunately, in this book it has not been feasible for its editor to make effective use of exteriors of houses as well as interiors and thus to show their relationships. However, there are very good and significant and characteristically twentieth-century reasons why this was not advisable. A great many of the rooms here published are in apartment houses, the exteriors of which are meaningless in relation to the style of the interiors—and often by every other standard of design as well. One expects when one enters a house to find an agreeable relationship between the design of its interior and what its architect made it look like outside; one does not expect to go into a large white clapboard house through a splendid eighteenth-century doorway and find oneself, as I once did on Long Island, in an elaborate Spanish mission interior, complete with rough plaster walls, wrought-iron candlesticks, and a fountain splashing into a tiled pool.

When one enters an apartment, however, one has no preconceived notion of what one will find. It could be argued that the very stylelessness of apartments is an asset, as a blank canvas is an asset to a painter, but unfortunately the builders of apartment houses have little regard for the shapes of rooms; they care only about the square footage of floor space. Who cares how high the ceilings are or if they are made into miserable, broken surfaces with awkward beams? Only the person who has to live with them or the decorator who has to eliminate or disguise them cares. In a very real sense many of the rooms in this book are not rooms in houses but cells in hives, and it is to the obvious credit of the decorators that they have created such elegance or casual pleasantness in spite of and not because of any assistance from the members of another profession who ought to know better, the architects.

In a sense this book itself is an ideal, Never-Never Land apartment house of a special sort. There is certainly no building in America, or anywhere else that I know of, that contains such a variety of pleasant rooms in such different moods reflecting such diverse personalities. There is no need for me to point out to the reader what he should look for in these rooms: the decorators have spoken for themselves. There are, however, a few obvious things that the rooms have in common.

The "period room," considered so fashionable only a few decades ago, has vanished, and so has the room based on a single fashion for a single country. There is nothing here like the rooms that reflected the Japanese craze that preceded the First World War or the Early American fad of the twenties in which a trumped-up kind of consistency substituted for imagination. The rooms that you will find here are, as I have said, eclectic in their styles and in the tastes they exhibit, and yet they seem to share a somewhat common tone of voice. They epitomize a kind of well-bred ease, a concern with objects that have quality whatever the era or place of their origin, and a delight in comfortable (not just ostentatious) luxury devoid for the most part of the stuffiness that used to be associated with it. None of these room is "modern" in the sense that "modern" is a period. It is a comment on the decorators, on their clients, and on design that so little furniture of the last three decades is to be seen in these pages and that so little of the spirit that characterizes the very best of contemporary architecture is here. No artist worth his salt, of course, strives to be "modern"; he strives only to do his best in the idiom in which he is most at home. There are, of course, many beautiful rooms that exude the spirit of contemporary architecture; none of them happens to be in this volume.

This is a book in which to go visiting. Unlike a visitor to a museum, you will not find yourself held back from sitting in the chairs or walking on the carpets. There are no velvet ropes or eagle-eyed guardians to restrain you. You can wander at leisure, relax, and in some of the rooms warm your feet before the fire. You can people the drawing rooms with your friends, sleep in the bed-rooms, dine in the dining room. The only person in this book, you will find as you turn its pages, is you. It is solely for your enjoyment.

—RUSSELL LYNES

The Finest Rooms

by America's Great Decorators

The Old
and the New

BY WILLIAM BALDWIN
OF BALDWIN AND MARTIN

I THINK IT CAN SAFELY BE SAID IN THIS CHANGING ERA THAT THERE HAS NEVER BEEN A TIME when Americans have had a greater scope in the field of decoration both old and new. There is an almost unlimited market of furnishings for us to choose from in the world of the past and in the world of today. I think, too, that more people are aware than ever before of what this vast choice includes. More people, and especially American women, have seen and read and studied the subject of furnishing and decoration than ever before. It is a great privilege but one that is also fraught with difficulties.

Certainly a great part of this awareness is due to the numerous magazines on the subject, to the newspapers—many of which have columns or articles on decorating—to the beautifully illustrated books, and to the many tours of houses as well as museums which so faithfully reproduce the past. In addition, due to the tremendous price range available, the possibility of possessing beautiful things becomes a reality for all tastes and pocketbooks.

It cannot be denied that magazines have contributed enormously in spite of the fact that the editorial pages of some are more than ever controlled and sometimes contaminated by the advertisers. This naturally does have considerable influence on what is illustrated, but all in all I believe that the influence is good rather than bad. However, the great problem that has arisen is the element and influence of "fashion." I do not think that the furnishing of a house or room should be approached with the same point of view as the purchase of a dress or a hat. Rooms should have far more permanent value than a seasonal excitement which can become passé in a year or so. Color should not be subject to the rules of fashion. Any color at any time may be used, especially if it is a favorite color of the person who is to live with it. Not long ago there was a national horror of orange. The color pages of magazines have done much to eliminate this prejudice, but almost to the extinction of red. Many women become afraid to use a color unless it is fashionable. This is, of course, absurd. I feel quite to the contrary and am inclined to avoid the current fashion. I dislike the idea of mass production in color or, for that matter, in any other aspect of decoration. I know, of course, that it is the way colors are used—the combinations and quantities—that makes the difference. But I feel disturbed when a client asks me if it is all right to use red when "*they* are using orange." Who are "they"?

In the city of Baltimore, where I came from, there is an old lady who has a fascinating house filled with a mixture of many kinds of furniture, all of which she loves. In the drawing room there is a set of four beautiful French chairs, and over a period of sixty years these have been re-covered from time to time from the same large bolt of pale blue silk she wisely purchased years ago. I always think of her and those blue chairs. Change would erase from my mind that charming memory, and I would hate to return one day and find them orange because orange is the "latest" color.

I know that a page devoted to decoration in the newspapers every day can indeed provide almost too much to choose from and can create a great deal of confusion. Today we have an embarrassment of riches, and that is where the advice of an experienced decorator can often save mistakes and therefore save money.

I use the word "advice" and use it purposely. Decorators should not be dictators. They should not impose their taste on clients; instead, they should endeavor to interpret their clients' taste to the best of their ability, a skill which develops through many years of practical experience. If they are objective the result can be personal. The room must belong to the owner, not to the decorator.

I am sure that what we remember most about rooms we like is the "atmosphere" or "mood" of the room. I am certain that this quality can never be attained unless there is an enormous personal manifestation. It must be suitable to the occupants both from the economic point of view and from the point of view of the use to which the room is put. The only trace of the decorator should be evidenced in the knowledge that the client has acquired through the long experience that the decorator has had, and this is quite different from the imposition of taste by the decorator.

I remember the day when I and the late Mrs. Ruby Ross Wood, with whom I had the good fortune to work for many years, went to tea at a friend's small town house in New York. We were both rather overwhelmed by the beauty and charm of our surroundings. When Mrs. Wood and I met at work the next day she said she was awake all night trying to analyze what it was that created the extraordinary atmosphere. The sitting room was furnished in very fine eighteenth-century furniture and the walls were hung with modern pictures, but the mood of it all came from the "pleasant memorabilia of living," a wonderfully expressive phrase of Mrs. Wood's. What she meant was that there was everywhere evidence of the life and taste of the woman who lived there—charming little wicker baskets filled with needlepoint hanging from arms of exquisite French chairs, and flowers in the most modest of wicker baskets on the finest of signed commodes and tables. Quite rightly, the modest little wicker basket in its way was as important as the impressive furniture. The flowers themselves were not affected by any rules for "arrangement," and seemed to have been placed lovingly and effortlessly.

On the question of flowers let me say that I believe it is a mistake to depend upon them to achieve the successful decoration of a room. Flowers today are too expensive for most people to acquire in any large quantity unless they have a garden or greenhouse. The great English decorator, the late Syrie Maugham, once told me that flowers must be thought of as "gravy." Certainly the beauty of fresh flowers does add immeasurably, but we do not want to have a room die with the flowers. I must admit that my criticism of much of the decoration of houses in Florida and California is that too much there depends upon the use of flowers and tropical plants. If you have ever been in Palm Beach off-season, at the time when the great palms and ficus plants are boarding at the florists for the summer, you are undoubtedly impressed by the complete collapse of the rooms. I do not think that this should happen, nor do I think that the formula which involves the use of plants to this extent is good decoration. Any room must be good enough to hold its own without them.

I feel strongly that no room should ever be entirely finished or "done." There must always be leeway for the room to grow, by the purchase of a piece of furniture better than the one originally owned, or by the addition of objects of beauty or utility purchased by the owner from time to time. However, the great risk of easy travel today is the almost irresistible lure of foreign bazaars, where much which looks lovely there may look unhappily out of place when ripped from indigenous surroundings and placed among unsympathetic strangers.

I will even go so far as to say that I approve thoroughly of permitting the wrong note in a room in order to achieve the personal quality, particularly if it is something loved by the owner or something which has the sentimental value of having been inherited. I love the look of a piece of furniture which seems to have been "brought down from the attic." I do not strive for perfection itself, since I know that perfection is virtually unattainable, and if it were attainable the result would be rather chilly. I really do prefer the wrong note to the obviously impersonal note. I like eccentricities, if they are the eccentricities of the owner. And I do not necessarily believe in throwing out everything and starting from scratch.

To return to the element of fashion again, the snobbism in taste for paintings today is due entirely to it, and has resulted in a colossal bore. Many people insist upon hanging walls with second-, third-, or fourth-rate examples of great Impressionist masters simply because of the signatures they bear. Actually, very often these pictures may not even be authentic. Certainly it is a lovely experience to see a picture, be seduced by it, and discover it has been painted by an unknown artist. This reflects the personal choice of the owner and shows that he or she is completely free from the influence of the fashion of the day. To be quite frank, I do not feel that anyone has the right to possess paintings, furniture, or objects unless he loves them.

At one time the deservedly much-admired Elsie de Wolfe waged a campaign against pictures. I am certain that she did this because she wished to rid the walls of the bad pictures which were the fashion at the time she began her brilliant career. We have luckily discarded this rule, but now it appears to be the rule that we *must* have pictures, which seems equally wrong. You must have them if you want and love them. I admire art-consciousness, but I deplore those who say that you must have this or that school, especially if the collecting is to be done by a decorator and arranged in one fell swoop by her or him. Any collection of anything must certainly be made by the collector himself, as he is the one who will have to live with it.

I approve of clutter if it is the true taste of the person who has brought it about, but if it is dictated from afar it becomes an affectation. This little rule works in reverse as well: it is sterilization to insist that a client who loves things be surrounded by empty space. Love of space can be very beautiful, but if it is not from the heart it is death. One important thing to avoid is the deep-freeze atmosphere of the museum. I am sure that all of us have come to the entrance of a room and have been stopped from entering it by "the rope that isn't there." As we approach a room it should lure us to enter and sit in it. The period room is for museums only, as it is impossible to make such a room personal. In addition, there is nothing in such rooms of the age in which we live today. There is nothing creative about them, and they can be assembled by any normally intelligent person who reads books or visits museums—and has the wherewithal. I much prefer a room decorated in the taste of the person who is to live there to the austere and forbidding atmosphere of an all-French room or unadulterated Williamsburg restoration.

I cannot conceive of any room that is to be lived in today without the use of upholstered furniture. The late nineteenth century brought this great luxury to us and we have never ceased enjoying it, and most of us spend much of our lives sitting on it. When buying it is a wise investment to have the best custom-made upholstered furniture because it lasts much longer than the average department-store equivalent, and today it is not really much more expensive.

Like the signed picture, I dislike the importance attached to signed French furniture. If there is a choice between a signed and unsigned piece, most certainly the winner should be the one that is more beautiful and suitable to the surroundings in which it is to be placed. Also, if it is a chair, I cannot overlook the important element of comfort.

Now, how do we proceed to bring about this personal result?

First of all, I believe in a mixture of everything, and by that I mean a mixture of all nationalities, old and new. I know that antique furniture brings a quality to a room that nothing else does. I also know that some modern furniture, carefully selected, is good and will continue to be so and become the antique of the future. All the antiques of today are the survivors of yesterday, and there are both good and bad examples among them. It should be remembered that not all antiques are beautiful just because they are antiques. I know that it takes a trained eye to discern good and bad in what is being made today. And there is nothing more dangerous than acquiring something—anything—just because it is different, a novelty. Quite likely the novelty of today will become the bad taste of tomorrow. It makes me very sad to see people, as I have seen them, invest a lot of money in a "conversation piece" which actually does provide something to talk about at the moment, but becomes unmentionable, or should become so, at the end of a year. I would like to see the owner try to sell it for even half the sum he invested in it! Many of these conversation pieces are made from things which have been forced into uses other than those originally intended. I do not like a teapot made into a table lamp or a stove made into a standing lamp. There is really no good reason for it, practically or aesthetically.

Most people who have seen a lot of houses and who care a lot about them agree that the greatest that have been created are the wonderful English country houses of the eighteenth and nineteenth centuries. The houses of the British Empire were filled with examples of every kind of furniture: French furniture of the most magnificent quality bought during the auctions at Versailles after the French Revolution, lacquer from the Orient, the great imaginative furniture and architecture of Italy, as well as the great examples of England's own cabinet work. These houses were always added to with beautiful examples of what was being done at the time. In these English houses all things were brought together from everywhere in the Empire. We today can assemble just such things from the "empire" of our markets. When the time came, the English added the luxury and comfort of upholstered furniture. Incidentally, it is an interesting little side note to remark how charming a pair of French chairs looks in an otherwise all-English room, but how completely ill at ease a pair of English chairs looks in a French room. In such a mixture there is the mixture of values as well as of styles. On a table we will find objects of great material value next to objects of sentimental value. Never hesitate to put the photograph of a friend side-by-side with the finest Meissen if you wish to do so. There is a beautiful house on Long Island where the walls are filled with a large collection of beautiful French Impressionist paintings hung above low bookcases built in the early part of this century. On top of the bookcases are masses of photographs and sketches and flowers, all personal, all loved. If you are in this room before the arrival of your hostess you will feel her complete personality, her whole life, expressed in it.

As to the arrangement of furniture, the primary element should be comfort. Every chair that is meant for reading should have excellent light, and there should be a table nearby—not too high, not too low—for cigarettes, tea, or a drink.

For the same reason it is wise to have a good reading light and a comfortable table beside the bed in every guest room. There should also be sufficient space on the table or commode for the guest to place his or her personal belongings. Besides being arranged for comfort, furniture should be placed so that there is the greatest possible flexibility, with chairs that are light enough to move easily. These should be chairs which when moved do not upset the arrangement of the room. I have sometimes seen a room after a party appear more charming in its disorder than when the chairs were aesthetically fixed by some brilliant floor plan. It is quite necessary to fasten furniture to the floor of a yacht, but it is a sad thing when someone asks you in your own room, "May I pull up this chair?" as though he were afraid to disturb the entire setting.

In most houses where there is a living room and small library, the library is the room that is most used. Very often the living room is not entered except for formal occasions, for wedding receptions and funerals. Yet a great percentage of the budget has probably been spent on the furnishing of this large and usually unfrequented room. No room can possibly have any atmosphere unless it is used and lived in. I have often suggested to clients that they put the television set in the big room so that the family is drawn there.

As to color, today I feel much the same as did the decorators of the eighteenth century. Color should be strong, fresh, and vital. We have been led up the garden path by imitations of what the eighteenth century has become rather than what the eighteenth century really was when it was new. I can make this point clear by asking anyone to look at the underside of an English needlepoint rug. The yarns are brilliant in color, and it is only the feet of generations that have exhausted it. The eighteenth century was a bold, tough period, and nowhere do we find faded, dying colors which have become so only after living over two hundred years. In the 1920s it was considered vulgar to have pure gold leaf on moldings because it was new-looking. When there were gold moldings they were painted with radiator paint and antiqued, which made an ugly color. Fortunately we are now rid of that affectation. In the many recently restored small rooms at Versailles and in all good English rooms as well we find the glory of pure gold leaf. Also, I would like to make a plea for brass and ormolu, which was never meant to be dirty and should be kept properly polished and shiny.

I believe that we are forever indebted to Matisse, the greatest decorative painter of our century, for completely emancipating us from Victorian color prejudices. His palette is everywhere in chintzes and silks of today, and is revealed as well in the attractive prints used for women's clothes. It seems almost unbelievable, but I can remember when pink and red flowers were never mixed!

In every room something modern can work an enormous difference. Most people do not hesitate to hang modern pictures on the walls of a room furnished with antiques. And a few often have the courage to add new furniture to old. This practice is especially desirable for contemporary design. I always prefer furniture of contemporary design to reproductions of antiques which have little value aesthetically or intrinsically. I know that even in the most extreme modern house the introduction of something from the past makes the difference between personal and impersonal rooms. A brilliant example of this is the glass pavilion of the modern American architect Philip Johnson. Standing on an easel is an enormous seventeenth-century French landscape by Poussin. It adds a quality that could not possibly exist in a contemporary picture; it is a classic link with the past in a beautifully classic modern room.

In the contemporary house of the Texas architect Hugo Newhouse, an extraordinary change was made simply by the introduction of four painted Venetian armchairs around a table. Before their appearance, the house was furnished entirely with contemporary furniture with extremely straight lines, the total effect being rather like a series of sticks. The graceful, gently curved lines introduced by the Venetian furniture enhanced at once the perfection of the classic modern lines of the house.

Another example of mixing the old with the new is the case of a client who during her married life had assembled a remarkable collection of Queen Anne furniture. She decided to build a house in the country and wished it to be extremely modern. When she asked me to come to see her she was completely honest; she told me that it was to be an interview and that I was among three decorators that she had sent for. After considerable conversation and a thorough inspection of the plans, she timidly said to me, "I don't suppose you could possibly use my Queen Anne furniture." I said that I would not be interested in doing the house unless we did. The result is that the bold, warm, personal collection of late seventeenth-century English furniture complements the house and makes it belong to the client in a way that no other pieces could have done so effectively.

The reverse of this is to be found in the case of a very French eighteenth-century bedroom belonging to an older woman in a New York apartment. She has an unusually fine collection of Louis XV and Louis XVI furniture. However, she wished to have with it fresh color, new paint, and a general change in the "antique" atmosphere that the room never had before. As a complete extension of this wish, a parquet floor in the Versailles pattern, but made of creamy-white vinyl, was also installed.

If a client wants a nineteenth-century Gothic library, it is up to me to create the best nineteenth-century Gothic library ever done, whether I like it or not. Or if a client has built an ultramodern house, it is up to me to furnish it to the best of my ability, taking all his or her wishes into account.

There are a couple of little vulgarities in decorating to which I hope nobody will ever succumb. One is the use of false books and the other is the use of a fake fireplace. I feel cheated by false books and I feel that a false fireplace in a room is like a body without a heart.

There is a very simple creed to follow when you approach the furnishing and decoration of a room:

Something to sit upon—which must have beauty and comfort; something to look upon—which must reflect the personal taste of the owner; and something to put upon —which means tables of comfortable height, conveniently arranged.

As a final word, I must say that architecture comes first, then decoration. I admit that very often today we are obliged to substitute decoration where there is no architecture, as in many of the apartment buildings currently being built throughout America. Nobody wants to eat a cake that is badly baked, even though the icing is pretty. The elements of proportion and scale are necessary before decoration is applied. Decoration is not the end, but the means toward the end. The house should be complete—and that means good housekeeping and good food as well. All this can be realized only when the client and the decorator have reached a happy relationship, and, if they have, the final result is bound to be one of endless pleasure and the feeling of well-being.

OPPOSITE: In this handsome country library in Georgian style, the decorators have used brilliant green wool plaid for the chairs and curtains and plain green for the sofas.

The transformation of a banal hotel sitting room in New York into a personal and domestic room resulted in the Proustian, turn-of-the-century setting shown on these two pages. The walls are hung in brown and pink paisley calico. The Bessarabian rug is patterned with Blackamoor heads, and the extraordinary chandelier is Venetian.

A large-scale, classically proportioned drawing room in a Long Island house. Blue and white chintz is almost everywhere, and the complementary shades of blue of the chairs and pillows are re-emphasized by the brilliant blue of the porcelain lamps—an effective contrast to the glowing patina of the wood.

Fashion designer Mollie Parnis's drawing room, made for parties, for pretty women, and for comfort. The severity of line of the French furniture is made gala by the use of gay colors.

A classic English hall in a great country house on Long Island is enlivened by red serge curtains, a Bessarabian carpet, and a chair covered in a contemporary interpretation of a Queen Anne documentary design.

For the furniture and curtains—a red, brown, and cream overscaled English chintz, strong enough to withstand the power of a magnificent early nineteenth-century English needlepoint carpet was used in the living room of this Vermont house. The picture at left is a painting by Mary Cassatt, the one over the mantel is a Manet.

Three rooms in the same house at Greenwich, Connecticut

OPPOSITE: A seventeenth-century East India Company print is used in a man's guest room. Green raw silk covers the Edwardian tufted chair.

This staircase hall, designed in the 1930s, remains fresh and pertinent today. Lacquer, a black and white still modern carpet, Dutch chairs in quilted beige linen, a remarkable beige floor in patterned stone, brilliant emerald-glass sconces—all contribute to the timeless decoration.

OPPOSITE: 1830 Lammermoor romanticism comes to life in a small guest room measuring only fourteen feet by twelve. The bed is hung with white organza, and the bedspread, also white, has embroidered green tassels. The tartan carpet is black and white and the green of the dressing table, bedside table, and windows accents the clover-leaf wallpaper, which is of recent design.

In the library of Cole Porter's New York apartment, brass and leather are combined. Leather is used behind the brass bookcases, old leather on the Regence chairs. Here modern bookcases and old furniture, and a large collection of books, encourage an atmosphere of ease and comfort thirty-one stories above Park Avenue.

A Door Always Open

BY ROSE CUMMING

J HAVE OFTEN BEEN ASKED TO WRITE A BOOK, AND I WOULD LIKE TO DO SO, BUT I PROBABLY never will, for I just do not seem to have the time. However, I am very happy to contribute a few pages here about myself, my experiences, and my approach to decorating. I won't promise that some of my remarks won't seem a little irrelevant to the main theme of this book, but I hope the reader will enjoy agreeing or disagreeing with my views about things in general and my specific feelings about what does and what does not make a house look beautiful.

Quite apart from writing a book, an article, or even a letter, I never really seem to have time for anything—even to buy a new pair of stockings—although, quite honestly, I'd rather do almost anything than buy a pair of stockings, because this means going to a department store, and I detest department stores. They are so impersonal, so regimented, and I am a nonconformist. It's the little shops, the old shops, that I most love, where I can poke about here and there, discovering beautiful things, odd things, and sometimes the occasional bargain that everyone loves to come across. The rarest treasure I ever unearthed was a lovely string of jade beads which I bought in a second-hand clothes shop for twenty-five dollars and which was eventually evaluated at six thousand. I must say this made me rather happy.

OPPOSITE: Sunshine streams through the large windows of this New York drawing room, reflecting on the polished floors and mirrored walls. The high-ceilinged, sixty-foot room is kept in good proportion by the adroit use of the tall Coromandel screen at the far end, and by the Louis XV chandelier. The boule writing table at one of the windows is set at a slight angle to help break up the extreme length of the room. (House of Dr. and Mrs. Russell Cecil.)

I am a shopkeeper at heart, apparently, and I have run a shop for over forty-five years—although of course I've been decorating, too, since the day I took my first job and started sorting samples. While there is always plenty of excitement in decorating rooms and helping others to do so, somehow the excitement of keeping a shop is different: there is always something going on, somebody new coming in, the chance—sometimes the excuse—to seek out, to handle, to learn about, and to enjoy every kind of antique and work of art; and there is always some new challenge—especially if you have a door always open.

When I came to America during the Great War, I was on my way from my native Australia to England, where I was to be married. But when I got to New York I discovered there were no passages for women available at that time on the sailings to England and I would have to wait a long time. Lunching one day with an old New Yorker, Frank Crowninshield, the editor of *Vanity Fair*, I told him that I couldn't bear sitting around doing nothing and that I was going mad with boredom. "Well, what would you like to do?" he asked. I replied quite desperately that I didn't know. "I'm perfectly useless," I said, "I don't know how to do anything." "Well, perhaps you would like to become a decorator?" he suggested. "Perhaps I would," I replied, "but first tell me what is it?" In Australia we only had people who covered chairs and made curtains, and when Mother needed anything like that done she would call Beard and Watson, Upholsterers. But as for a decorator, we had never heard of such an animal. "Crownie" introduced me to Mary Buel, a famous New York decorator at that time, and I found myself with a job. Very soon I knew that this was to be my greatest love.

That was a long time ago, and since it has been said about me—only recently—that my age is unguessable, I shall only say that it *was* a long time ago! Since then I have decorated countless houses in New York, and a great many out of town—in San Francisco, Burlingame, Detroit, Minneapolis, St. Paul; on Long Island, in New Jersey, Florida; and occasionally in New England, though not many up there, where I think people prefer to do everything themselves. I have also worked in England, Australia, and New Zealand.

I quickly learned what it meant to be a decorator, and in 1929 I wrote the definition which I think still applies: "Interior decorating is the frivolous sister of the architectural profession. It requires primarily that one be an expert in color, design, period, and the placing of furniture. Most of us have added some knowledge of architecture to our equipment as decorators, so that being conversant with the laws of proportion, line, et cetera, we can intelligently interpret the original design of the architect. A decorator should, in addition, be blessed with a sixth sense—a kind of artistic alchemy which endows the articles of furniture with that elusive quality of livableness which transforms houses into homes." No amount of training or schooling, I believe, can teach you this. Either you have a flair or you haven't.

I love everything that is beautiful, no matter whether it is fish or fowl. My loves are passionate and legion. I dearly love Gothic, and early English furniture of the sixteenth and seventeenth centuries; I love all early Oriental furniture and art with the exception of Indian; I adore Chippendale, the Louis XV period, Austrian Baroque, and early painted Venetian. In country houses I like French Provincial and Kitchen Colonial, with the old oak or pine, and the sense of quiet and peace that somehow comes with it; I am especially fond of early Victorian, with those lovely Belter couches and chairs; then, too, I like Regency and Directoire furniture and the beautiful wallpapers of that period. I love old mirrors, glittering chandeliers, and highly polished floors where the old wood and the furniture always look their best. Samarkands, Isfahans, Aubussons, and Savonneries are my favorite carpets; in fact, I love all lush things—not, however, to the exclusion of simple things, provided they are well designed and placed in appropriate settings. I must add to my list of loves birdcages—particularly Oriental ones—and smooth silky fabrics, and jade and mother-of-pearl. More than anything else I love the possessions people have either inherited or are going to hand down to their descendants, for it is these that give a room a particular personal character, a feeling of tradition and continuity, a fully justified link with the past. With passion I love pure colors: fresh, brilliant, and clear colors like cyclamen white, all tones of blue, lilac and violet, blue-green, brilliant purples, yellows and bronzes, and my own particular combinations of jade and blue. Another of my special whims is collecting—I collect frogs, mice, monkeys, horses, dogs, cats, fruits, and vegetables (ornamental ones, of course), also pictures made of cut papers, wax figurines, snuffboxes, glass paperweights, period inkwells, and miniature furniture.

It is probably already quite obvious that my list of loves could go on for pages which no one will have the patience to read, so I might interject here a remark my sister once made which sums things up rather succinctly. "Rose," she said, "there are only three things you really love: you love everything to look frightfully fresh, frightfully clean, and frightfully well cared for." I believe she was right. I do like everything to be clean and gleaming; parquet floors that you can see your face in, highly polished tables that reflect the lovely objects placed on them. In my opinion one of the greatest pleasures of having old furniture and beautiful things is seeing them in a house that is well cared for. A house always seems to smile when it is clean and polished, and I think we owe this to the furniture to soothe its aged feelings, so to speak.

No one ever asks me about my dislikes, but I am as loyal to these as I am to my loves. To begin with, I dislike most muted and muddied colors. Then it seems to me that a great deal of my decorating life has been blighted by the presence of pseudo-beams in ceilings that were never supposed to have them—seven here, fourteen going the other way, and seven more a different way. What kind of a drawing room can you make out of this? In a genuine old country cottage or house where the beams are structural and necessary, this is a different story. I am depressed by figured wallpapers unless they are exceptionally beautiful, like silver paper, or old Chinese paper. I cannot imagine spending every day of my life watching a small ship sailing around a bad wave, and I wouldn't want anyone else to have to, either. Coffee tables are another hate of mine: there were no such things in earlier periods, but apparently it is a kind of animal that has to exist today, and if it absolutely must be fitted into an antique room, I never cut down or adapt a table; I find a piece of old lacquer, or something similar, and create a lovely old table around it. Lampshades are another hate—chiefly, however, because it is a terrific effort, and a bore, getting just the right size, right shape, and right-colored shade to fit the right lamp at the right height. Admitting my weakness, I always leave the lampshades to the maker, who is an expert and knows more about them than I do. Besides that, I don't understand electricity, and whenever possible I much prefer to use candles, which give a much warmer and more flattering light to the table and to the room as a whole. What is prettier than a room glowing with candlelight and a fire? When candles are not possible, it is advisable to use indirect electric lighting, which helps eliminate the deadliness of too many lampshades in a room.

" 'Ere-to-'ere," or wall-to-wall, carpeting, to me is unforgivable and not to be tolerated except in bedrooms or on poor staircases. In my opinion, the effect of yards and yards of heavy wool on a drawing-room floor is suffocating. If you have a pretty floor, why not show it to advantage and use an occasional rug? If you don't have a good floor, in the end it may not be any more expensive to install one than to resort to wall-to-wall carpeting, especially as this, in time, will have to be replaced.

I have many hates in modern architecture, and I believe they are shared by many people. Actually, I'm not interested in modern architecture at all and don't understand it, but when asked which modern structure I like most in New York I will say it's the Lever Building. At least it has *some* romance. Most modern apartment buildings are disasters with small rooms and thin walls where one must live in constant conflict with one's neighbors' bathroom noises and kitchen smells; modern rooms which have no fireplaces and have oppressively low ceilings are not for me. One may be consoled by a view and by the luxury of washing machines, but for me this consolation is not enough. Surely there must be some possibility of injecting a new thought or design into these modern buildings in which, when a door is opened, everything looks precisely like hundreds of thousands of others and where halls with hundreds of doors leading into other exactly similar apartments give the feeling of walking through a mental institution.

When I am considering decorating for a new client, I like to know immediately what colors she likes, what period she prefers, and what kind of atmosphere she wants me to create for her. It is also helpful if the client reveals as soon as possible how much she really can afford to spend. Many is the time a woman has come to me giving the impression, either by her appearance or by her conversation, that she wants something close to an ancestral hall and then shows me an eight-foot-ceilinged room with no fireplace and with a carpet bought from the last tenant, with perhaps a few curtains thrown in for good measure. At other times someone walks into the shop creating a very modest impression, and it turns out that not only does she want an ancestral hall but she really can afford to have one! In return for this initial frankness on the part of prospective clients, I am equally frank with them. I make my likes and dislikes quite clear from the beginning and we either see eye-to-eye or we don't. I tell her that I like houses, or rooms, that present a potpourri of many styles and periods—a harmonious, romantic, lush, and beautiful mixture of everything. This is the style that I helped create for America's aristocracy in the Golden Age of the Twenties, and it is the style I still stick to whenever I can today. I plead with her to start with a beautifully proportioned room with high ceilings and a fireplace if she can afford it. This is half the battle.

OPPOSITE: Mirrored panels were installed on the walls of this landing to give the illusion of space and depth. The impact of the early Chinese temple pagoda, eighteenth-century chandelier, and Chinese marble goddess is made even more dramatic by their repeated reflections. (House of Rose Cumming.)

This extraordinary room was created by Rose Cumming as the result of a spur-of-the-moment reaction against the usual conception of prettiness in decorating. Sinister, ugly, destructive, or macabre objects and decorations are used, yet so skillfully and colorfully that a dramatic effect is created as well as a room where a man could live and be comfortable. The setting is dominated by a superb painting by Jean Baptiste Oudry, painted in his black period, depicting a deep pool with wild ducks and a vulture poised for attack. Audubon prints above the couch depict rats, weasels, and other creatures of prey; the tiles around the fireplace are decorated with plates from an old book on venomous snakes. The leather boar at the foot of the side chair (near the book case with a vase of early swords from Spain), is a seventeenth-century gout stool, and the lampshade is an Indonesian parasol. Bronze Ming and Meissen monkeys flank the sofa. Old saris veil the windows which are screened by harem doors from India. The rugs are seventeenth-century Corsican with tufts of cyclamen pink. A warrior's head from New Ireland stands on the top of the bookcase menacingly surveying the whole room.

In the drawing room of Miss Cumming's brownstone house a romantic aura of the eighteenth century is created. The early Ming hand-painted wallpaper panels and beautiful parquet floors provide a fitting frame for the Louis XV pieces, most of which are signed. The Chinese chandelier is a rare eighteenth-century one made of papier mâché.

'A' bedroom belonging in time to the rich, improbable style of the twenties. The walls gleam with metallic blue-mauve paper, and silver and blue lamé hangings echo these colors. On either side of a sixteenth-century Portuguese iron bed, and at the foot of it, are silverplated Moorish tables and stools believed to have been owned by Catherine the Great. The child's bed, serving as a low table, is eighteenth-century Persian, and the carpet from China provides a luxurious covering for the parquet floor.

That is why so many of those old houses in England and France are so beautiful—they are lovely to begin with, and you really hardly care if there is any furniture in them at all. Of all the graceful features, I believe that a high ceiling is the most important of all. It makes every woman look beautiful when she enters the room; but if a low ceiling practically scalps her, she comes into the room looking like a pigmy.

For me, decorating is a trial-and-error thing, like trying on hats until you find the one that fits. First comes the room; next the collection of suitable furnishings which I place in the middle of the room. Then I start pulling and dragging everything back and forth, trying objects here and there, until I find the exact place in the room where this or that piece looks best—and there it stays forever. I've been in my own house, for instance, for almost a quarter of a century, and I've never moved one stick of furniture. The hat fits, so why change it? Some clients have different ideas and would prefer to work from a prearranged plan or a blueprint. I don't agree with this method, and if they persist I send them to someone else. In real decorating there are no precedents. Every house, every room is different, and you cannot be sure of the exact position any object should occupy until you try it out.

I have strong convictions and a strong will to support them, and this frequently leads to controversy with clients who also have strong convictions and strong wills of their own! There have been, therefore, many amusing experiences and some, I regret to state, rather bitter ones, during the past forty-five years of my decorating life. There was, for instance, the time when, many years ago, after completing a simply magnificent room, I lost that particular client because though she paid the bill for forty thousand dollars without a murmur, she deducted seventy-five cents for my chauffeur's lunch! And then there was the extraordinary episode of the seventeenth-century lamp. One's love of beautiful things is never-ending, and I simply can't resist them, so in those early days, as today, I am afraid that when I fall in love with a beautiful thing I buy it and bring it back to my shop. At the time of which I am speaking, I had some very beautiful early seventeenth-century lamps on consignment from Spain. One day a wealthy and influential New York lady came into my shop, saw one of these lamps, and asked the price. I told her that it was "two-fifty," so she said she'd buy it and take it home with her. The next morning, when I came back to the shop, to my astonishment I found the lamp stuck in the wastepaper basket which had been put outside with the garbage to be emptied. There was no note, and no word ever came from the lady herself, and the mystery deepened. And then one day I heard of a funny story that was being told at dinner parties in New York about the famous Mrs. X. It seems that she had bought a lamp in a Madison Avenue shop and when, on opening the box at home, she had found among the wrappings a bill for $250 and not for $2.50 as she had thought it cost, she sent it back in outrage. It was difficult for anyone to imagine how this very grand lady could possibly have thought that any lamp—never mind an exquisite seventeenth-century piece—could cost only $2.50!

There are countless other stories, however, to balance ones like these; stories which have contributed to making my life as a decorator a wonderfully exciting and elating one. For instance, there was the time of the robbery, when I first started off in my own little shop. The rent money for the first months had been loaned to me by my sister Dorothy, as I had absolutely nothing to my name. The furniture had been lent to me on consignment by Schmidt Brothers, simply out of kindness in order to help me get started; I had been allowed to choose from their floors all the pieces I wanted, and these were in the shop at the time the burglars broke in. When I came back to the shop the following day, exactly four months after I had opened, every stick of furniture had been stolen except for one couch. This was a disaster of the greatest magnitude, and I could not think of a single thing I could do to recover myself. Everything in the world I possessed was gone, and I felt there was no one to whom I could turn for help, as everyone I knew had already helped me. But then along came a messenger, that very day, with a letter. "Friends of yours are distressed to hear of this thing which has befallen you just as you are beginning on your career. We are enclosing a cheque for $5000, and if at any time your loss is less than at the moment [the papers had said that it was close to $5000] you can return the difference to the Lincoln Trust Co. on 28th Street." It was for things like this that I grew to love America. I *never* knew who this wonderfully generous person was until twenty-five years later.

Then there was the gentleman who came to my shop door late one evening, in a Rolls-Royce with two men on the box, and asked me if I would consider decorating an apartment for an invalid friend of his. It was one of those lovely apartments in an old house on Madison Avenue, and I fell for it immediately. "My friend is very delicate," he said, "and can't be burdened with any details of any kind, so I want you to do it as though you were doing it for yourself, but as quickly as possible." And so I did. I spared nothing and put in it the most beautiful Chippendale and Louis XV furniture I could find. The colors I used were yellows, flames, and browns. At that time I had a staff of thirty, and worked with wonderful laborers and tradesmen, so the job was completed in a little over two months. When I called the gentleman and told him that the apartment was now ready for his friend to move into, he asked me if I would play hostess on the day she arrived. I willingly agreed to do so because I really cared terribly about the whole project and had put all my heart and soul into making it exceptional. When the moment came, I was there waiting for her, and he was there too, waiting. The fire and candles were lit, and flowers were gaily arranged everywhere. Then the door opened, and the lady wasn't an invalid at all: she was an extremely beautiful young woman. She stood in the door taking the whole thing in, then she moved across the high-ceilinged room to the fireplace, put her arms on the mantelpiece, then turned slowly around to face us and said, "If in all the world there was anything I ever wished for or desired, it is all here. There is nothing missing—it is all here." Then she burst into tears; so did I; so did he—we all howled our heads off. Several years later on one of my visits to London, I was invited to a ball at the house of the Duchess of Rutland, where an American woman was being sponsored by the Duchess and being received into London society. At the top of the stairs, to receive the guests, stood the Duchess, and next to her, beautiful as ever, stood the same woman. When I got to the top of the stairs and close enough for her to recognize me, she turned as white as death; I realized that some dreadful tragedy must have happened, so not by even a gesture did I betray her.

And so the years crowded on, and times and circumstances changed for us all, but as I continued "keeping shop" and decorating houses, the touching and wonderful stories continued to grow. I should like to end this brief account with the following story which, since I am a sentimentalist, moves me to this day. Having been forced to move my shop three years ago from

Madison Avenue to my present location on Park Avenue, I received many nice letters telling me of how people felt and wishing me success. One day, shortly after the move, as I was arranging things in the shop window, a young man went by, stopped, and retracing his steps walked through the open door. "Oh, Miss Cumming," he said, shaking my hand, "I'm so glad. It's wonderful to find you here. I didn't know *where* you were. Everyone has been asking."

A few days later I received a letter from him. He wrote, "Dear Miss Cumming; I'm writing you this letter and am not putting my address at the top because I have no axe to grind whatever, but I felt that I really had to write you and tell you what you have meant in my life. When I came to New York as a boy of 19, I was very poor, and I always loved to look at your windows. But more than that, I was so often hungry and seldom could have anything to eat at night, and whenever this happened I would think to myself: 'What will I do?' So I'd go and look in your windows, and come away refreshed. These are my memories."

I was surprised and greatly touched. I have never seen him since, and I wish I knew his name.

As you can see—there are all kinds of things that happen if you have a door always open.

A small dining room made important through the use of fine English furniture. The chairs are Hepplewhite, the sideboard is Sheraton, and the unusual hectagonal dining table is eighteenth-century country Chippendale. The red Chinese lacquer cabinet adds a bright note of color.

Color plays an important part in this high-ceilinged library. The walls are emerald green, the sofa is brilliant purple, and the Portuguese Queen Anne–style chairs are red and gold lacquer. The focal point of the room is the beautiful Queen Anne secretary, also of red lacquer, as are the two consoles. The painting by Ramsay is of the young Maitland who became Admiral Maitland and later took Napoleon to Elba.

BELOW: Richness and delicacy are in full evidence in Miss Cumming's small blue and gold drawing room. The eighteenth-century table inlaid with boss, the Adam consoles, the Louis XV couch, the harpischord with black keys, and the chandelier —said to have belonged to Czar Nicholas II—these all seem at home with the silk rug and Raeburn paintings.

Many different figured materials are successfully combined in this living room. The Bessarabian rug has a *tête-de-nègre* background and designs in faded reds, blues, and greens. The chairs by the fireplace are covered in antique crewel work, and the barrel chair at left is covered in' a blue chintz matching the walls. (Apartment of Mr. and Mrs. Myron A. Wick.)

BELOW: A Chinese paper with yellow, pink, and white flowers and soft blue-green foliage on a pale green background covers the walls of this bedroom. The curtains, bed, and chaise longue are in bluish-green materials. (Apartment of Mr. and Mrs. Harold S. Vanderbilt.)

Forty Years
of Decorating

BY MARIAN HALL
OF TATE AND HALL

Decorating! A word that includes so many things. Designing rooms for people who start out from scratch; helping clients who begin with ugly rooms in a house or apartment and wish them to be transformed into something charming and livable; suggesting, helping, buying, choosing, measuring, encouraging, and sometimes having to be discouraging. It is a varied, fascinating, and at times frustrating profession.

I don't believe in false modesty, so I can say quite frankly that I wouldn't have been helping people decorate their houses for over forty years if I didn't think and weren't encouraged to think that I was good at it. However, I agree with all the other decorators who are worth their salt that a house or apartment should never look as if it had been designed and furnished by a professional. Taste is a highly personal thing, and the place that a person lives in must reflect this taste and look as though he or she had created the rooms. Nevertheless, for a home to become as charming as the owner has envisioned, and also to be practical and comfortable, the knowledge and experience of a decorator who has faced every sort of architectural and furnishing problem are often required to help put things in order. In other words, it seems to work out in life that two heads are usually better than one.

One of the nicest things ever said to me in my decorating career came from a client of mine who remarked, "I've always admired Mrs. X's house very much, and I only heard the other day that you had been working for her for years." I consider this the highest kind of praise a decorator can receive.

As in all forms of art, the hard and fast rule without exceptions cannot exist in good decorating. Almost anything can be done if it is handled well. A bedroom, for instance, can be equally charming when wallpaper, curtains, bed drapery, and bedspreads carry the same pattern or a combination of patterns and plain colors. The guest room on page 70 (center right) follows the first plan; the effect is warm, gay, and—despite the repetition of the same pattern—not at all monotonous. A different room, featuring a variety of patterns, is shown on page 58 (top). This living room has two figured Bessarabian rugs, each with a different pattern. The curtains and some of the chairs display the same figured chintz, which was chosen to go well with the color of the rug. Other chairs in the room are covered in a chintz with a smaller design of appropriate color, and still others are covered in the crewel work. The result is lively yet harmonious.

It is often said, both in and out of the decorating world, that furniture of different countries should not be mixed. This is a mistaken notion, another hard and fast rule; the sooner it is forgotten the better it will be for all of us. Nine times out of ten it simply does not apply. America is a polyglot nation, and it is just as appropriate to mix furniture of different countries as it is to bring together people of different countries and let them get on with each other. Any disharmony can be rectified by removing an offending chair, table, or footstool and placing it, if worthy, in another room. I also believe in mixing different periods of furniture when the occasion calls for it. I like furniture of all periods and of every country; that is, I like the best examples that each has produced, whether American, English, French, Italian, Spanish, or Dutch. Like everyone, I have my favorites and lesser favorites, and my special preference happens to be the classic French. I don't expect everyone to agree with this choice; in fact, I hope they don't, because it would be very dull if everyone liked the same things equally well. In the decorating world there are so many beautiful things to choose from, so many different things, and so many ways of combining them that one of the great joys of visiting houses is to see not only how well they have been decorated but how differently people have expressed themselves in their individual surroundings.

The choice of a color scheme for a room is very important. There are so many possibilities here that at times it can become bewildering to the average home owner. In the end, however, the choice will usually reflect the owner's favorite colors, which in turn will reflect his personality to a considerable extent. One of the colors I like most to use in a dining room is green. I agree that green in any shade provides a good background for china and flowers and for the varied colors worn by ladies seated around the dining table. But for this reason to make a hard and fast rule that all dining rooms should have green walls would be stupid, to say the least. I myself have done dining rooms in many different colors and many different styles. One of the most charming of these featured soft pink and off-white French paneling; another was in shades of white, another predominantly red. As always, it depends on the taste, the furniture, and the demands of the individual involved.

One of the things that make decorating such a fascinating profession is the endless variety of people one works for and the different types of work one is asked to do. For instance, nothing could be more different from decorating Sherry's restaurant at the Metropolitan Opera House in New York—certainly the most challenging job I ever had to tackle—than decorating, say, Arthur Sachs' dining room on the French Riviera. The Metropolitan Opera House was built in 1883, and the restaurant dining room I was asked to do had a great deal of ornamental plaster work on the ceiling and walls. A room of this sort is of course furnished entirely with tables and chairs, and the only possible chance of decoration is on the walls and ceiling. I felt that the walls should be made to look like those of a ballroom in the 1880s, so I had them covered in American Beauty color flock wallpaper, which gives the effect of damask. The plaster work was painted the color of the paper and picked out in gold. The Opera House owns a large number of life-size portraits of the great artists who have sung there, framed in heavy gold frames, which look extremely handsome as they stand out against the richly textured red background. The long side lights are gold too, and gold and crystal chandeliers hang in glittering cascades from the ceiling. The whole effect is lush and brilliant, a room where opera lovers can dine and drink between acts amid an old-world atmosphere of elegance and gala.

The Sachs' dining room, in their Cannes villa, presented a quite different kind of challenge, but a serious one nevertheless. The architect had placed large windows on two sides of the room which gave one the impression of being out of doors—or almost. To emphasize this idea and to make the room even more sunny and gay I suggested bird murals set in latticed panels and the use of painted iron garden furniture which complete the pleasant open air illusion.

One of the most exciting opportunities I have had in recent years was that of working from the very beginning on the New York apartment of Mr. and Mrs. Carl J. Schmidlapp. The Schmidlapps bought the space before the building was started, and, working with the architect, Mott B. Schmidt, we were able to plan completely the disposition of the rooms, the sizes, partitions, and wall spaces as the owners liked.

Mrs. Schmidlapp and I found a beautiful oval Adam room at an old and distinguished furniture dealer in New York. This (page 69) was installed as the reception room, and in the dining room next to it we carried out the Adam theme, copying the palm-tree motifs from the beautiful Adam tearoom at Moor Park in Hartfordshire, England.

Another unusual job that came to me recently was the decoration of a combination wine cellar—and bomb shelter. The cellar was well supplied with whisky and gin, but the principal stock consisted of the great wines of France, so we decided that the chandeliers and chairs should be *tricolore*, leaving the bottles (as can be seen in the illustration on page 70, bottom right) to take care of the walls in a rather unique fashion.

Although I love originality and love furniture with fantasy, such as Chippendale mirrors with carvings of squirrels and foxes, gold console tables with cranes or sheaves of wheat at their bases, and the blackamoors that play such a large part in Venetian decorations, I have never been enthusiastic about what are known as "amusing rooms." I feel rooms should be comfortable and personal and serve the purpose for which they are designed. They can be cheerful and gay or serene and quiet in mood or they can be as original as anyone desires— just so long as they are tastefully done and are not self-conscious. Some "amusing rooms" may not actually be unlivable, but the trouble is that no joke can bear telling every fifteen minutes.

Even too much smartness is a doubtful asset. The reason for this is that smartness, which usually means the employment of some kind of gimmick, is largely a matter of fashion, and when the style changes the room looks shopworn, out of date, stale! People say of last year's clothes, "You wouldn't be seen dead in them," and you still have to be seen alive in your room. If you cannot throw away everything you have and redecorate every year it is well to avoid extremes.

I have written these notes in the first person but fortunately Diana Tate, who has been my partner for over forty years, and I see eye-to-eye. If we didn't do so we wouldn't have been able to work happily together for such a long time. Had I been able to make her write this piece, she would have said the same things I have said here, only very much better. The accompanying illustrations include her work as well as mine.

OPPOSITE: The white walls and curtains in this morning room provide a perfect contrast for the needlework rug with a white floral design on an eggplant background. Most of the French antique furniture is painted white, and the two Louis XV *bergères* are covered in pale blue satin. (Apartment of Mrs. Carl J. Schmidlapp; see also color pages 68 and 69.)

The blue and white drawing room in the Washington house of Mr. and Mrs. George A. Garrett contains four fine eighteenth-century decorative paintings and French chairs and tables of the same period. The walls and curtains are both off-white, a color repeated in the Aubusson rug with its rose and blue flowers. The superb Adam mirror, one of a pair, has a sapphire blue glass frame with a carved gilt frame.

Two rooms in the apartment of Mr. and Mrs. Landon K. Thorne.

The dining room was inspired by the one at Pitzhanger Manor in Ealing, England. The walls and curtains are white, the rug is black with a bright green and white pattern, and the Chippendale chairs are covered with emerald-green damask. In the living room the antique *boiserie* is painted pale green with moldings picked out in white, providing a classical background for the eighteenth-century French furniture covered in white and pink damasks and brocades. The green, white, gold, and pink rug is Bessarabian, made for the European market in the eighteenth century. The screen is white Chinese lacquer.

LEFT: The bedroom features an eighteenth-century bed, a fruitwood commode, and a chaise lounge covered in velvet.

OPPOSITE: The antique Adam oval reception room was brought to New York from Northhamptonshire, England. The walls with set-in mirrors are robin's-egg blue; the floor is antique parquet. The chandelier is Russian but goes well with the English candelabra.

BELOW: The living room has antique Louis XVI *boiserie* walls and furniture covered in various white materials, some with patterns that pick up the color of the moldings and the pink of the antique Ghiordes rug.

Rooms in the New York apartment of Mr. and Mrs. Carl J. Schmidlapp.

ON THE OPPOSITE PAGE:

TOP LEFT: An old French wallpaper from Tours establishes the mood and color of a country dining room. The antique table is French and the provincial chairs are French and Italian. (House of Mrs. Carl J. Schmidlapp.)

TOP RIGHT: Early American paneling, rough white plaster walls, early maple tables, hooked rugs, and soft chintz colors all contribute to the quiet and restful atmosphere of this country library. (House of Mrs. Carl J. Schmidlapp.)

CENTER LEFT: The owners of this house in Pennsylvania treasure their collection of prints, jugs, lamps, and mantel ornaments with a cock-fighting motif. Many of these are arranged in the handsome library with its lacquer walls of unusual color. The figured linen curtains have a fighting-cock design. The modern rug comes from Portugal. (House of Mr. and Mrs. Edward T. McLean.)

CENTER RIGHT: A charming guest room with curtains, chaise longue, dressing table, bed drapery, and bedspreads in a chintz that matches the wallpaper. (House of Mr. and Mrs. John M. Schiff.)

BOTTOM LEFT: The living room of a pool house has sectional sofas placed near the door leading to the pool. In winter the sofas are arranged by the fireplace. The chintz design pictures a French waterfront town, and the modern hooked rug has a rope-and-anchor motif. (Pool house of Mr. and Mrs. John P. Humes.)

BOTTOM RIGHT: This combination wine cellar and bomb shelter has walls of natural brick, a stone floor, and oak ceiling and wine racks. The *tricolore* scheme includes a tole chandelier painted to simulate red, white, and blue ribbons.

Private Worlds
of Retreat

BY MRS. ELEANOR S. BROWN
OF McMILLEN, INC.

Gertrude Stein once wrote, "France has scientific methods, machines and electricity but does not believe that these things have anything to do with the real business of living. Life is tradition and human nature." As we know, the French have always taken time to live, but to us in another land and in an age of advanced scientific progress Miss Stein's statement seems perhaps somewhat old-fashioned and unreal. When we witness such marvels as satellites, man's emergence into space, and now the imminent possibility of a conquest of the moon, can we, dare we, believe that life is tradition and human nature?

It is my deep feeling not only that we can but that we must! For all the spectacular wonders that appear with dizzying rapidity from day to day, for all the almost superhuman achievements of man, for all the complexities of our civilization, there must be in our private worlds a counterbalance. Knowledge based on tradition plus fortitude and daring carries scientific man forward. Knowledge based on tradition plus an imaginative and sensitive concept of his private world makes this possible. For without the private world of retreat man becomes virtually an unbalanced creature. Human nature is equipped to adjust, but can change little. Man is still a creature requiring comforts and even luxuries, of a rather prescribed and traditional nature. How then are we to achieve this counterbalance?

Houses and clothing answer the human requirement for shelter and provide the personal realm. They express an individual or national conception of an ideal of beauty in color and form. Our mode of dress, though varied to suit the demands of the day and the fashions of the seasons, certainly reflects our degrees of taste, personal preferences, and even personalities. Even more profoundly, the manner in which we live and the quality of our surroundings are reflective of our social, intellectual, and cultural status.

OPPOSITE: Louis XV Italian chairs painted blue and gold and covered in white damask are in gay contrast to the yellow walls of this dining room. Added interest is introduced by the colorful eighteenth-century rug and the glittering facets of the Venetian mirror and crystal candelabra. (House of Mrs. Adolphus Busch.)

Dress is the public expression of private man—influenced to a great extent by fashion, whereas a house is but the normal expression of his intellectual concept of fitness and his aesthetic idea of what is beautiful. Love of beauty and the desire to create it is a primal instinct in man. It is right that we should wish to live in a manner that is in keeping with our own time in history. Our houses should reflect our own personal philosophy and in turn to some extent the philosophy of our age, and reflect, in the same way that all art forms in ages past have, the record of social structure encompassing the religious as well as the political aspects of the development of civilization. The primitive graphics or prehistoric art of man before 20,000 B.C. were documentations of his life or his visual means of communication, as can be seen in decorated caves. The highly ornamental and decorative qualities of Egyptian architecture, sculpture, and minor arts must be recognized as symbolic expressions of a people's philosophy, government, and religion.

So it has been down through the ages. Man has moved through the long passages of time digesting, recording, changing, but always leaving in his time and place the records of how he lived and why. What will the records of our own time show? Are we too often inclined to think of art in terms of pure decoration rather than as a vital part of our everyday lives?

Our lives today are the result of a rich and growing artistic and intellectual heritage. Our houses are a part of our time. Whether the house itself is old or new—whether it be from another period in time or whether it is today's best architectural expression—matters little. A lovely old house that knows the mellowness of time in its walls and in its furnishings remains vital through the recognition and acceptance of the best of today's arts and sciences. By the same token a contemporary house that ignores all vestiges of the past in order to express a purely modern philosophy runs the risk of becoming a stagnant document of its own time, lacking in vitality and becoming just as boring and unnatural as any "antique" period brought intact for today's living.

There is nothing more trite than a set period. And when I say this I am not questioning the splendid, beautiful rooms in old houses. They were made for the houses. What I am questioning is the trite settings of past eras which always resemble something out of a museum. We do not want trite reproductions. The late eighteenth-century room in Aix-en-Provence with its lovely *toile de Jouy* on the walls, with its provincial furniture, does not look so well and is far from appropriate when reproduced in apartment 16R. Fortunately, however, there is now an intelligent trend away from many such abuses of the past.

There can be no life without change to some degree—be it ever so subtle. Change may be recognized in the most sophisticated sense as development—development of taste, of quality, and of personality. All rooms express these things and all of these are relative. Let us consider these separately.

OPPOSITE: An octagonal bedroom with walls covered in beige self-stripe silk makes a perfect setting for the brown and gold Regency tester bed said to have been executed for Prince Albert at Brighton. The four-tier tables and Foliot bench are rare Louis XVI pieces, and the C. M. Le Clerc acajou cylinder desk, of the same period, has a stand desk section as well as the usual pull-out sitting section. The mahogany Directoire chair is one of a set of four. Mounted on an orange stand are seventeenth-century ivory and bronze *doré* urns; the wood polychrome madonna is fourteenth century. The bedspread is deep gold velvet; the tester, pale yellow silk.

A small library with a soft blue *boiserie* and off-white moldings. The mantel, blue-velvet-covered stool, needlework rug, and English chair are all eighteenth century. On the mantel—at either side of the Renoir—are Waterford crystal candelabra, and over the sofa is a painting by Monet. (Apartment of Mrs. Marshall Field.)

OPPOSITE: This living room, with a twenty-one-foot ceiling, occupies what were originally two floors in an apartment house. The problem presented by the fourteen windows was solved by closing off all seven on the upper tier and three below, and by draping the curtains over the walls to give the windows better proportions. The furniture is eighteenth-century English, French, and Italian with a red lacquer secretary of the Queen Anne period at the far end. (Apartment of Mr. and Mrs. Diego Suarez.)

The beautiful shades of antique Louis XVI Aubusson rugs dictated the color scheme for this drawing room—off-white damask for the *bergère*, brown and yellow upholstery, and an antique off-white linen tablecloth embroidered in beige and light browns. (House of Mr. and Mrs. Diego Suarez.)

Taste is relative and is the sum total of the intellectual and emotional experiences of the individual. Taste, in order to be positive and vital, must be exercised and developed. Taste is changeable and is influenced by environment. A highly cultivated taste, a taste that is knowledgeable and eclectic, is likely to be exciting and provocative, a personal taste at its highest level.

Quality is relative and is defined by degree of excellence. The quality of an object is evaluated in terms of the honesty of the material employed for its creation—the excellence and purity of its design, and its suitability for the purpose intended, be it a telescope or a tea table.

Personality is relative and is the result of purposeful control over positive and negative natural forces. Personality is an active force and as such is expressed either positively or negatively. A rich personality is capable of profound expression while a barren or negative personality, lacking in imagination, cannot be expected to surpass its capabilities.

To develop in taste, quality, and personality one is obliged to respect the past, accept the present, and look with enthusiasm toward the future.

Today there are men and women working in every field as free agents in the art world who produce for us designs and techniques of extraordinary quality and beauty. The quality of contemporary work will continue in proportion to the degree of cooperation between our capable designers and patrons interested in quality who are themselves courageous in ideas. We might ask how the work of the contemporary artist and craftsman is to be employed as we endeavor to assemble or re-evaluate our houses and our rooms. The mood of a room must dictate. Every room has a mood or personality—sometimes latent—and it is this that one desires to develop. Some rooms are rich in physical structure and are comparatively easy to bring to life, while others lack distinguishing features and sometimes even have blatant faults. Such rooms require more skill to assemble and are more of a challenge to one's creative talents.

And then the eye must select. The selective eye must be an experienced eye, an eye that knows the genuine pleasures of harmonious colors and textures, of sensitive line and proportion, of the play in contrasts of light and shade. The selective eye must see beyond immediate limitations, recognize possibilities that a fertile imagination suggests, and translate the difference between the genuine and the false. The selective eye must also be quick to respond to those things, tangible or intangible, that are the elusive—perhaps even witty—ingredients of a happy room. The contemporary eye combines objects and materials from the past with objects and materials of the present, not because of force or fashion, not because of friend or neighbor, but rather because of an eclecticism, the result of one's own experiences and one's own knowledgeable taste.

The artist then serves as our guide and our source of supply. The artist and the craftsman have worked almost from the beginning of time with the patron in the creation of houses and rooms in which to live and live more opulently—rooms that have reflected the wishes and personality of the patron and rooms richer and more vital because of the trained, knowledgeable, and

OPPOSITE: The Georgia pine dining room at Blair House, the President's Guest House in Washington, D.C., is painted antique white and has white curtains trimmed with blue and white fringe to tie in with the set of blue and white Lowestoft presented by Mrs. Edgar Garbisch. This generous gift enables Blair House to serve dinner for twenty-four guests. At the left, balancing the twelve-paneled seventeenth-century Coromandel screen of the K'ang Hsi period, is a magnificent seventeenth-century blue and white crystal mirror which hangs over the buffet.

sensitive eye of the artist. Particularly has this been true in those cases where the patron has had the courage and the imagination to stimulate the creative powers of the artist, thus helping to express through the talents of another his own individuality. It is in this manner that the contemporary artist and craftsman can collaborate with us as we endeavor to create rooms that are reflections of ourselves and of our society—rooms of great quality that are a dynamic expression of a taste which is active, alive, exciting, and never negative. With such positive taste the old and the explosive new go hand in hand.

Contemporary paintings and sculpture, for instance, seem happily at home with furnishings of the past. Fabrics of contemporary colors and textures seem suitable and appealing on old chairs. Old patterns seem excitingly fresh when rejuvenated by a contemporary palette. The magic of modern lighting and ventilation enhances rooms otherwise traditional. The settled, comfortable look of beautiful upholstery makes otherwise austere rooms more cozy, and adds to rooms of clinical structure the traditional qualities of charm and comfort. Active positive taste demands a constantly fresh appraisal of familiar forms. Such an appraisal is a constant re-evaluation of one's own pattern of living—discarding, collecting, and discarding again, holding on to those things that add quality, beauty, and pleasure to one's life, disposing of superficial impediments.

How one is to achieve rooms of harmony, vitality, and beauty is a personal thing, the result being—and rightly so—that each is a mirror or reflection, so to speak, of the individual. Rooms do have personality: some positive and some negative. Our goal, of course, should be to create rooms that are suitable to our own mode of living, that meet our personal requirements of comfort, that function for the purpose for which they are intended. Aesthetically, we should settle for nothing but the best. We must demand that all things that come into the realm of our private world, our houses and our rooms, be a delight to the eye and a satisfaction to the intellect. We must recognize that pure art is part of the necessity for individual expression, although not always requiring communication, and that functional art must communicate but need not, thereby, suffer in quality.

These are our homes, our private worlds; let them welcome us and make us happy. Let them grow and not stagnate. Let them be the mirrors of our personalities and not the reflections of others'; let them be splendid achievements of self-expression—achievements of this counterbalance so necessary in our world today. Our neighbor's world is his own world, and our worlds are our own, and though they must associate agreeably they need not be the same. We must have the courage of our convictions about our own worlds but see to it that they hold all the delights rather than, like Bluebeard's Chamber, all the horrors.

EDITOR'S NOTE:

Mrs. Eleanor S. Brown is the head of the firm of McMillen, Inc., which consists of many decorators whose work is shown in this chapter. Mrs. E. Everett Smith is responsible for the rooms on pages 78, 84, and 85; Mrs. Marion K. Morgan for the rooms on pages 76 (bottom), 77, 83 (top), 86 (top left), 90, 91; Mrs. Irene M. Walker for the rooms on pages 76 (top) and 81; Mrs. Virgil Sherrill for the rooms on pages 84 and 85; Mrs. Russell W. Davenport, associated with McMillen, is responsible for the rooms on pages 75, 83 (bottom), 86 (left center and bottom), 87, 88-89, 92, and 93.

Dark green walls give this gun room a strong masculine feeling. The sofa and upholstered chairs are covered with off-white twill embroidered in various tones of green. The other chairs are done in lighter yellow-green raw silk. The old English hunting scene over the marble mantel is by John Fernley. (House of Mr. and Mrs. Robert Winthrop.)

OPPOSITE: The Louis XV *boiserie* in Mrs. Anne McDonnell Ford's drawing room, painted a soft yellow with moldings picked out in old white, makes a perfect background for her fine and rare collection of furniture, the majority of which consists of signed pieces. The outstanding Louis XVI mahogany and bronze doré desk in the foreground is stamped I. H. Riesener and bears the inscription V.R. (with crown) 1866, Windsor Castle. The pair of Regency carved and guilded fauteuils on either side of the fireplace and the matching *bergères* are signed Cressent Ainé. In the niches are Mrs. Ford's collections of yellow and blue Meissen (circa 1725-1745) and Rose-Pompadour Sèvres.

An Old World atmosphere pervades this library in Newport. The impression is enhanced not only by the portrait over the fireplace but by the old books which are so much a part of the room, by the solid and comfortable arrangement of the furniture, and the cut of the striped curtains. The bronzes on the mantel are by Herbert Hazeltine. (House of Mr. and Mrs. Sheldon Whitehouse.)

RIGHT: A contemporary studio-living room designed for a man with a large country place who wanted a small *pied-à-terre* in town. The apartment reflects its owner's interest in big-game hunting and race horses. The rug is a zebra skin; the glass table tops are supported by nineteenth-century Indian teak elephants and the pouf in the background is covered with monkey fur. The tapestry is by Dom Robert; below it, the red lacquer cabinet houses a bar, a record player, and a television set.

Four rooms from the Rosedown Plantation in St. Francisville, Louisiana, owned by Mr. and Mrs. Milton R. Underwood.

BELOW: Most of the furniture in the dining room was original to the house, although many of the chairs, assumed to be Duncan Phyfe, and part of the table, had to be rebuilt. The punkah frame is also original, but part of the needlework eagle was reworked; it follows a design by Audubon, who tutored the children of William Turnbull and his wife, the builders of the house. The original mirror over the fireplace reflects one of the two Sully portraits of the Turnbulls in the room.

In the blue and gold music room, a rosewood piano made by Chickering stands under a portrait of a member of the Turnbull family painted by Audubon. The harp is of honey-colored maple, striped in gold and black.

RIGHT: The walls of the master bedroom are covered with a copy of the original paper in pinks, blues, and soft reds. The massive rosewood bed has a canopy in pink-stripe silk, and the antique lace bedspread is lined with pink. The Louis Philippe chairs are still covered in their original printed velvet.

OPPOSITE PAGE: The entrance hall. Blue and gold wallpaper, made by Dufour and Leroy in France in 1828, duplicates the old paper, which was damaged beyond restoring. The paper dado is a copy. The stair, made of Santo Domingo mahogany, stands as firmly as it did over one hundred and twenty-five years ago.

Louis XVI hallway. (Apartment of Mr. and Mrs. David Granger.)

A color scheme suggested by the Portuguese fireplace tiles.

A long room in the Park Avenue apartment of Mrs. Skinner Smith is arranged to allow for both small- and large-scale entertaining.

The *boiserie* from the Basque region of France, the parquet de Versailles floor, the Savonnerie rug, and the Louis XVI mantel, obelisk, clock, *bergères*, and side lights create an authentic French atmosphere in this New York apartment.

The problem of housing a writer's large collection of books in a limited area is ingeniously solved in this house in the Berkshires. The far side of the living room is thirteen feet high, and a catwalk is suspended from the ceiling by thin iron rails so all books can be easily reached. At the right and back of the free-standing fireplace is an eighteen-foot built-in desk. The light forest-green ceiling, between the beams, repeats the textured fabric on the upholstered furniture. The octagonal Renaissance table at the left holds a blue Persian wine-jug lamp and more books. (House of Mrs. Russell W. Davenport.)

Three rooms in the Grosse Pointe house of Mr. Henry Ford II.

In the morning room (left), soft yellow-green walls, a neutral rug, and gay quilted chintz curtains and upholstery provide a light and cheerful atmosphere. The painting is *"Paysan en Blouse Bleue"* by Cézanne.

OPPOSITE: The soft pinks, blues, and off-white of the Adam rug set the tone for all the furnishings in the main hall of Mr. Ford's house and provide a lustrous background for fine furniture and paintings. The curtains are pale green faille with a deeper green and blue border. The gilt Adam chairs (from Battle Abbey in England) are covered with an off-white and sharp green cut velvet copied from an eighteenth-century design. Off-white silk with green and off-white gimps and tassels cover the banquette. Candelabra on the Adam consoles and the superb chandelier are both antique Waterford crystal. Over the fireplace Manet's "Portrait of Guillaudin."

Mr. Ford's fine collection of old books has found exactly the right setting in this beautifully paneled library. The Grinling Gibbons carvings over the mantel, the wing chair covered in antique Hungarian needlework, and the Queen Anne coral lacquer secretary add notes of elegance and comfort. The painting over the fireplace is *"Pagans et le Père de Degas"* by Degas.

Beige and deep yellow toile covers the walls and furniture of this tiny sitting-and-guest room. The chimney, built at an angle to add to the wry aspect of the room, has a Restoration mantelpiece of *brèche d'Alep* marble. One Directoire chair may be seen here; another against the opposite wall accompanies a tall *bureau-secretaire*.

A man's bedroom in the country is lightened by the unusual combination of yellow walls with white woodwork and shutters. The bed, designed by McMillen, Inc., to retain the early feeling of the house is covered in a printed yellow, white, and orange linen which is also used on two armchairs. The bureau and the bed tables are English; the mirror above the bureau is made from a frame used by New England fishermen for weaving nets. An orange stool at the end of the bed adds a dash of bright color.

The private drawing room on the second floor of the White House was designed for the late John F. Kennedy and Mrs. Kennedy. The windows have yellow taffeta curtains and command a spectacular view, over the gardens and lawns, of the Washington Monument. (The room is also shown in color on pages 106-107.)

First Memories

BY MRS. HENRY PARISH II

I THINK EVERYONE MUST HAVE A FIRST MEMORY OF SOME HOUSE, SOME ROOM, A VIVID PICture that will remain deep down in one forever. Rightly or wrongly, it is there. It may be in one's subconscious, influencing one's likes and dislikes through life. It is true one does progress, one does change. Inevitably, one follows the trend of the day; but it is that first memory of a room that counts, that in some way helps to shape one's feelings and thoughts.

My first conscious realization of a room was when it was taken from me. I was six. It was my family's sitting room in the country. The walls were white, the floor covered with pale yellow matting, a needlework rug of strewn white roses tattered and worn. The furniture was wicker painted white, upright and stiff. The backs and seats of the chairs had hard cushions, padded and buttoned. I remember the buttons would pop off, leaving little white strings. I felt sorry for the buttons and would try to put them back on. The material of the cushions and of the curtains was a heavy white cotton printed with vines and roses. The window seat was cushioned in the same material, with white borders, starched and fluted.

The mantel, also painted white, had a deep organdy-and-lace ruffle tacked onto the edge of the shelf. The gold clock with two heavy columns stood under a glass dome; I remember it struck on the half-hour. On each side of it were white candlesticks with angels clustered at their bases.

The lamps were twisted glass with shades made of paper. The shades were the feature of the room. My father had made them, cutouts of lacy designs of flowers, birds, and clouds. I remember my mother saying, "Please put a wash of pale pink inside them."

Years later in Paris I was to hear these same words of advice echoed. It was not long ago, when Madame Ritz herself conducted me on a tour of the Ritz Hotel. She said to me, "In doing a room, you have only one rule to remember: always line your lampshades with pale pink."

But back to my room, of which I remember every detail as though it were yesterday: tables of wicker, some covered in lace to the floor, others just bumpy, and of course white. The bowls of flowers, filled every day with roses from the garden, looked like the curtain and cushion material. Family pictures in silver frames were everywhere, especially on top of the eye-level bookcase. The wood basket with a big hoop handle was always full; the doorstop was an iron dog painted black.

The desk was a white table. On it were a big green blotting pad with silver corners, an upright silver paper-holder with three partitions, ribboned book markers, silver paper cutters, sealing wax, a glass inkstand with a silver top like a shining ball, and penholders of ivory, tole, and gold, the quills lying alone beside them. The desk chair was white too, but made of cane and garlanded with flowers around its curved back; on the seat, again, a thin, frayed pad, this one of pale blue damask. On the round table next to the stiff sofa was a silver bell. To this day I can see and hear it, summoning someone in the house—maid or child, we came.

The tea tray of white wicker on a two-wheeled cart had a glass top with the same curtain material underneath. To my utter amazement, the silver kettle on its stand could lean forward to pour. The china was white with a gold rim; the food, bread and butter with a little jam. Always, the smell of that room was a potpourri of lavender in a bowl.

I shall never forget the day of the "change"—the excited anxiety of my father, the day the room was to be thought of as "forgotten," the day my beloved room was destroyed. Everything in it, dear to me, was to be taken away, and the room was to be transfigured for the wonder of all to see.

From the time my room was destroyed until the First World War was over and I was eight years old, the "change" had crept all through the house, upstairs as well as down. Pine, maple, and cherry beds had taken the place of our white iron or brass ones, and each had its canopy and chintz spread. I can even remember the pattern of my mother's spread. It was quilted and had a gravestone with two cypress trees; cows were grazing in one corner and a kitten, for some unknown reason, was playing with a ball.

New ornaments had infiltrated the house—wax flowers, Staffordshire animals, loving china couples, tufted flower pictures, and many oil paintings of valleys and streams. There were comfortable overstuffed sofas and chairs, the first I had ever seen. The dining room table was cherry, the chairs painted black, with rush seats and gold decorations of fruits and flowers.

After I was nine or ten we moved, not for good but for a few months each year, to our new house in New York. Here was change, change indeed! A six-story town house with an elevator, paneled rooms, Adam mantels, a great curving stairway winding upward free from the walls and banked, step by step, with flowering potted plants . . . I think I was impressed, but never deeply touched.

In those days, people "did" their own houses, enlisting the services of very grand shops like Lenygon & Morant, the Schmidt Brothers, Mrs. Hooper, and French & Company. It was they who undertook to install the pine-paneled library from England, the white-and-gold-paneled drawing room, the mahogany doors, the parquet floors, the Queen Anne mirrors. From their own custom workshops they provided the carpeting, the damask hangings, the needlework rugs. Collectors and connoisseurs as they were, they found the furniture—lacquered consoles, inlaid sideboards, a magnificent breakfront secretary, drum tables, beautiful porcelains, four Adam chairs that stood around the card table, even the English portraits. "English, all English," were the words I was to hear so often from my father.

I was, however, deeply moved by one incident which concerned my own room, the only French room in the house. It was done in yellow flowered chintz and painted furniture, gay but very sophisticated—white wallpaper with little gold stars, parquet floor from our Paris apartment glowing with wax and age. Before the fireplace was an Aubusson rug, brown with pale flowers and blue ribbons. My mother showed the room to me with pride and joy. I hurled myself to the floor and sobbed, "You promised me pink!" I think it was the only time I ever saw my mother cry. . . . But there was, after all, something in that room for me : I had a window seat, to remind me of my old sitting room, lost when I was six.

My husband and I did our first house when I was nineteen, soon after we were married. We lived in a small white farmhouse with picket fence and apple trees around it. From my family-in-law's town house I had chosen, of all things, a suite of black ebony, sofa and chairs covered in blue Aubusson tapestry with pink flowers. There was also a rug to match. (Unfortunately, the children had been allowed to roller-skate on it.) I painted the ebony white and put white striped paper on the walls and used white mattress ticking for the curtains. In this room, where each side of the mantle was mirrored, I put two white sofas, a papier-mâché table with fringe (all these were especially made), and two white and gold console tables with marble tops.

Off the living room we built a small greenhouse with an old brick floor. We furnished it with a huge sofa covered with yellow, and dozens of pillows. Here two wicker chairs crept back into my life. This was where we really lived, with the flowers, the pots of bulbs, and the trailing vines.

Our bedroom was beyond the greenhouse, opening into it. It had a high tray ceiling, the walls dead white, the floor painted in cherry-red and white diamonds. The mantel was made of structural Steuben glass whose moldings were applied directly to the wall, which had been painted cherry red just there. The bed was covered with white silk taffeta with a border of flowers. Above the head of the bed this taffeta drapery flowed downward from a crown. I remember that the first night we spent there we kept the lamps lit because it was so beautiful.

I suppose all this must have looked strange in a little white farmhouse. It did puzzle people but, luckily, in the right way. My first job came soon after that. Not until then had I dreamed of decorating as a career.

We had heavenly years there, and were later to have wonderful ones in our New York apartments. But now our house in Maine is *really* home. I think I feel this way because it looks like the first room that I remember. Without my even trying, it just came back, even to the organdy ruffle on the white mantelpiece, the white painted furniture, the canopied beds, the quilted bedspreads, and my white wicker everywhere. (I tried a bolt of modern Swedish linen once. It's gone now because it just wasn't me.) There are the painted floors and bowls of roses from the garden. I realize now how much that first impression really meant.

Today when someone asks me to help create a room my first reaction, if I do not already know the person, is to try to feel out what he or she really wants the room to be and to understand, if possible, what "memory," old or new, has brought this idea about. I believe that when someone asks for help in planning and assembling a room, this person must have thought about it for many reasons. Something has been wrong with the room, or possibly it's just a change he wants.

My work has often been referred to as having the Undecorated Look. If my Undecorated Look has meant rooms that are personal, comfortable, friendly, and gay, I feel I have accomplished a great deal. Rooms should be "timeless." They should have as much imagination and warmth as possible. Each person's life differs from every other, just as people's needs are all different. If I can create for them a "living" room, I feel a true success has been achieved.

OPPOSITE: An entrance hall with a boldly patterned floor and a combination of French and Italian furniture. Beyond is the high-ceilinged living room shown in more detail on page 100. (House of Mr. and Mrs. C. Champe Taliaferro.)

This living room, which Mrs. Parrish created many years ago had a very personal collection of furniture and *objets d'art*, which were arranged in a delightfully fresh and imaginative manner.

A larger house built more recently for the Taliaferros contains much of
the same furniture seen on the opposite page. The same brilliant quality
of simplicity and light has been maintained in this new living room.

The dining room (above) shows an imaginative way of displaying fine porcelain. In an indirectly lighted niche brackets of various sizes are arranged to hold the individual pieces. On the opposite wall is a similar arrangement of brackets in a *trompe l'oeil* niche. The decorative plaster work is a perfect background for the English furniture, the Coromandel screen, and the silk Indian rug.

Three rooms in Mrs. Lytle Hull's lovely stucco house above the Hudson River at Rhinebeck, New York.

Of particular interest in Mrs. Hull's large drawing room is the use of soft colors—fresh lettuce green, soft mauves, pinks, yellows. The dramatic impact of the large-scale-pattern floor, ingeniously worked in a classic design of light and dark woods, is heightened by the soft, arabesque-design needlework rug. The unstudied assembly of furniture and objects helps to establish a mood of comfort and quiet elegance.

OPPOSITE: The view across the garden and river is of course a planned feature of the bedroom. An old botanical chintz covers two of the chairs, and another flowered pattern is used for the curtains. The bed has a headboard covered in a finely stitched soft yellow material. The latter is also used for the spread.

A bedroom of great feminine charm. The bed, of embroidered silk, is happily combined with delicate fruitwood furniture, charming porcelains and *objets d'art*, and a highly decorative painted screen.

The dining room in the same apartment contains an agreeable combination of French and English furniture. Over the large French mantel hangs a magnificent Chippendale mirror. An Aubusson rug is combined with an English table and French chairs, centered under the Waterford chandelier.

ABOVE: The simple paneling of this drawing room is painted soft green, a becoming background for an eclectic collection of French and English furniture, rare porcelain, and a particularly beautiful eighteenth-century Savonnerie rug.

LEFT: Flanking the wide recessed bookcases in the pale green paneled library are a painted and gilded barometer and a clock. Again, antique furniture of high quality has been arranged in a classic and comfortable manner.

The late President Kennedy's and Mrs. Kennedy's oval drawing room in the White House. Eighteenth-century French furniture is combined with comfortable upholstered sofas and chairs. The Louis XVI chandelier is bronze *doré* and rock crystal.

OVERLEAF: The drawing room of Mr. and Mrs. Henry Parish II is a romantic and inventive combination of furniture and possessions collected by the owners on both sides of the Atlantic. The room, used constantly for entertaining, is arranged in intimate groups for conversation. The large Aubusson rug, the variety of materials that cover the pieces of furniture, the juxtaposition of modern sculpture and paintings with a wide collection of antiques, immediately establish an unself-conscious style that is Mrs. Parish's "trade-mark."

OPPOSITE: The rough-textured walls, painted off-white, make a good background for Mrs. Vincent Astor's extensive collection of furniture, pictures, and *objets d'art*. The superb Aubusson rug, with its sky-blue field, is scattered with stars, and fat, fleecy clouds surround a gaily colored center bouquet of mixed flowers. A band of similar flowers borders the entire rug.

ABOVE: Mrs. Astor's library has light honey-colored paneling, an ideal foil for the brown-striped, multicolored chintz which covers the sofa (and several chairs which are not shown). The rug, strong in design though subtle in color, knits together the personal objects and antique furniture in a most agreeable manner.

OPPOSITE: The nostalgic assortment of furniture and objects is so completely suited to this Georgetown house that it seems that the room must always have existed as it is seen today. The colors are an opulent combination of rich, jewel-like hues—vibrant coral, sky blue, rich gold, and warm greens. (House of Mrs. Oates Leiter.)

In the house of Mrs. Thomas Jefferson Coolidge.

ABOVE: A large, luxurious bath and dressing room with painted furniture and flowery fabrics.

LEFT: A corner of the bedroom of the late Mr. Thomas Jefferson Coolidge, showing a collection of blue and white Thomas Jefferson Lowestoft china and a portrait of Thomas Jefferson. The eighteenth-century chair is English.

OPPOSITE: In the bedroom, a white bed is hung in hand-painted silk in shades of shell pink on an off-white ground. The unusual Louis XV painted desk has a bevy of small drawers and cupboards. Also against the far wall are two pictures representing rooms in Mrs. Coolidge's former Georgian house in Brookline, Massachusetts.

BELOW: Two views of the combination dining room and office in Mr. and Mrs. Bennett Cerf's town house. The folding shutters close at night to conceal the office, but when the room is used for large parties the desk is transformed into a buffet. A comfortable chair and small table are placed by the large window overlooking the garden—favorite place for breakfast and the morning papers.

This pool house belonging to Mr. and Mrs. Charles Engelhard is a pot
pourri of possessions—great masses of exotic plants and sporting trophies.

Cellar Sweeping
Was Not for Me

BY GEORGE STACEY

$\mathcal{I}$T MIGHT BE OF INTEREST TO THE READER, AND ALSO POSSIBLY OF HELP TO HIM IF HE aspires to be a decorator, if I start off by describing the beginning, and some of the more amusing aspects, of my own experience in the field.

After graduating, but only just, from the Parsons School of Design and after spending two summers in Paris, and, I fear, a good deal of time in between Stratford, Connecticut, at the age of nineteen I arrived at last at the moment of truth, when a job became something of paramount importance.

Somehow the school had managed to imbue in one the feeling that a decorator is a pretty important person—which is just as well when you are looking for work. During an eight-day voyage from Paris back to New York, I made up my mind that the one person I wanted to work for was Miss Rose Cumming, whose great flair for color and materials was established even then and remains undimmed today. No one who has seen or talked to Miss Cumming could manage, by any trick of the imagination, to think of her as "the girl next door," and by the time I actually arrived in her presence I needed a drink to bolster my rapidly collapsing ego. For some reason, and I suspect it was a mixture of kindness and pity, I was hired and told to report the next morning at her shop, which was then located on Madison Avenue in the fifties. All set to start right in on forty-foot-square Louis XV masterpieces of elegance, I was instead handed a broom and told to sweep the cellar. This task I performed with diligence all day long, and, not having much humor about it at the time, I decided that cellar-sweeping was not for me. Little could I

OPPOSITE: Detail of the entrance hall in Mr. George Stacey's apartment.

117

have anticipated that at the end of the Great Depression in the early thirties I would find myself a window dresser in a Philadelphia department store, my special field "kitchen equipment." Miss Cumming had recognized my forte at once.

From these experiences in my early working life I learned a great deal about the business of day-to-day living and working side by side with many different types of workmen which later made it easier for me to understand both my clients and the people of diverse skills who actually carried out the work.

And so it was that several years later through greater experience I was to amend my original estimate of the importance of a decorator, for I knew now that a decorator places somewhere after a psychoanalyst and a plumber—both of whom are rather more important in a crisis, although perhaps neither a psychoanalyst nor a plumber could produce an attractive interior, even in a crisis.

Skipping now to the post-Depression years, I was eventually offered a job in New York, and it was then that I really got started as a decorator, thanks to one person whose untiring help in finding clients for me resulted in a long and happy career. Without that help I doubt if it could ever have happened. As with any life, the outcome is generally due to a rare chance one is given; after that it is up to you.

I am sure that every decorator will agree with me that one of the first and most important things in this profession is to come to know and understand one's clients. This is the analyst side of it. One must know their interests and create as best one can a background in which they both look and feel their best and where their individual interests can best be reflected. One never need worry about expressing oneself; this can be left to the time when a client comes along who really has no interest in decorating: then one can really let oneself go. I am happy to be able to say that I have had very few clients who were uninterested in their houses, so I have not been put to the alternative test, and just as well—although it has been possible for me to work out this urge in one swoop as I was able to acquire a hundred-room Louis XIII château in France and in my spare time to decorate room after room at my own leisure.

Although it is important to do a job which looks as though a decorator had had very little to do with it—as though the room or house had already existed for some time—it is equally important to give the client the chance to take some measure of credit for his own very vital part in the creation of the whole, which certainly is his due. After all, you are in it as a business as well as because it is something you love doing, and not in order to collect pretty phrases.

One of the requisites of a competent decorator is real knowledge of period furniture of any country. It is, in general, a fairly complicated study involving research, comparisons, and a liking for both art and history. With this knowledge, and with a knowledge of color, any young decorator is, I feel sure, well on his way.

OPPOSITE: Two views of the drawing room in Mr. and Mrs. Ward Cheney's house in New York City. The yellow walls, satin curtains and the furniture covered in yellow, off-white, and brown merge with the browns and yellows of the needle-point carpet. The owner's large collection of rare eighteenth-century embroidered pictures contributes to the old world atmosphere.

Shades of blue, tangerine-pink, and white were used to create a colorful, light and airy atmosphere in Mr. and Mrs. Harold Guinzburg's New York house. The collection of books and fine furniture reflects the interests of the late publisher. Canvas covers the walls and Viennese drop blinds are used at the windows. The prie-dieu, *trumeau,* and occasional chairs are Louis XVI, the table is eighteenth-century English, and the rare black and gold lacquer pieces are Chinese.

BELOW: The uncompromising architecture of a modern apartment house is softened by white damask curtains and a beautiful eighteenth-century Chinese lacquer screen, divided so as to stand at either side of the fireplace and cover the two entrance doors. (Apartment of Mr. and Mrs. Ralph E. Ablon.)

In answer to the questions most often put to me about decorating, I would say the following. My favorite classic styles are eighteenth-century French, Italian, and English—in that order. I prefer painted French and Italian furniture to plain wood, and simple rather than elaborate design. I definitely believe in mixing different styles of furniture both in a house and in a room. One of the most common errors people make in decorating is trying to make a room perfect in all the details of a single given period, which inevitably results in a stiff and impersonal background. I am also frequently asked about color schemes suitable for specific rooms, wall-to-wall carpeting, and whether free-standing lamps should or should not all be arranged so that the illumination is at the same height in a room. My answers are: any color scheme in any room is permissible and acceptable provided it suits the owner of the house or apartment; in small, very cut-up areas wall-to-wall carpeting makes sense because it tends to minimize angles and to give a feeling of greater space; and free-standing lamps should be at approximately the same height in order to relieve an excess of conflicting shadows.

The question of what pictures to have, and where and how to hang them, seems to arise with persistent urgency. If a person is a collector, or has a good number of original paintings, there is no problem except as to how and where to hang them. They surely need not be hung according to any rigid rule such as keeping the frames level either at the top or at the bottom; this is a matter for individual preference and taste and may depend on how the pictures relate in color, shape, and style and the position in the room they are to occupy. As to where they should be hung, I prefer to hang them in groups rather than spread them around the room, provided the slide rule isn't used to determine their position. The individual eye should be the invisible "instinctive" slide rule. But if there are no original paintings, and the budget is limited, instead of using reproductions of good paintings I suggest purely decorative ones, or old paintings which are handsome or pretty but of little intrinsic value.

Floors are another important problem in houses and apartments alike. Personally, from the standpoint of beauty, I prefer *parquet de Versailles*, and then herringbone, or carlage.

When asked what I consider to be the most interesting and challenging decorating job I have ever done, I unhesitatingly reply, because it happens to be true: furnishing an old converted three-masted Spanish fruit schooner! And to the frequently asked question as to what originally prompted me to enter the field of decorating, my answer is of the simplest: curiosity. I would like to add—for the benefit and encouragement of young people who are thinking of entering the field—it has been wonderfully satisfied!

OPPOSITE: Two rooms in Dr. and Mrs. Leon Levy's Palm Beach house. TOP: A detail of the dining room showing a magnificent mantelpiece made from an early eighteenth-century over-door painted in black, gray, and gold. Six rare Empire silver gilt candlesticks add to the unusual character of the room. BOTTOM: In the living room, a magnificent twelve-panel eighteenth-century Chinese lacquer screen stands boldly against the far wall. A combination Louis XVI gilt clock and barometer hangs over a Louis XVI console. Two gilded *torchères* in the windows are English.

OPPOSITE: White and gold Louis XVI *boiseries* line the antechamber of the *Palais Princier* in Monaco, providing a fittingly ornate setting for the rest of the decor. The pink inlaid stone floor makes a subtle background for the white chairs covered in green velvet, the green embroidered cloth over the large center table, and the brilliant white satin curtains with green swags. A Louis XVI chandelier and wall lights cast soft illuminations at night, while in the daytime indoor plants soften the glare of the Mediterranean sun. (Prince Rainier and Princess Grace of Monaco.)

Deep talisman-rose damask curtains and chairs covered in bois de rose are in delicate contrast to the deep green walls and matching carpet of George Stacey's living room. The furniture spans French history from the Louis XV boule table under the bas-relief to a Directoire screen in back of the sofa. Imaginatively combined with these are a Chinese inlaid coffee table and a painted leather Italian screen. The large Empire painting over the mantel is by a pupil of David.

The pale gray-blue walls, printed taffeta curtains, bed, and chaise longue in this apartment bedroom need no compensating colors to relieve the muted color scheme. Through the window is a view over New York's East River. The lovely eighteenth-century English mantel and painted Louis XV *trumeau* contribute to the elegant and quiet atmosphere.

The drawing room in Miss Ava Gardner's house in Madrid. The center sofas (covered in brown) were placed, back to back, with a table between them, in order to break up the great length of the room and make two distinct groupings. The walls and silk curtains are gray-mauve, the carpet white. Two of the four Louis XVI gilt chairs are covered in red silk and the other pair are in yellow, which helps to distribute the color emphasis throughout the room. Eighteenth-century silk tablecloths in yellow-green achieve the same purpose. The lamps, objects, and pictures are also eighteenth century.

The predominant Empire style set by the painting over the fireplace in this room (see pages 126-127) is carried out in the bust of Jerome Bonaparte, the paintings, the *bibelots,* and the striking groups of classic urns on the huge English Regency bookcase. The graceful side chair at the right bears the stamp of the Petit Trianon. Candles flickering in the gilt sconces are softly reflected in the green walls.

Three photographs taken in George Stacey's impressive Château de Neuville. ABOVE: A corner of the large drawing room. The Louis XVI bookcase at right is painted pale blue and the chairs are covered in brown, yellows, green, and red. The *boiseries* are pale gray and the curtains are of yellow and brown taffeta.

CENTER AND ABOVE: White walls, a green carpet, and a gilt Louis XV armchair covered in cherry-red cotton repeat the tones of the chintz on the Louis XIII bed in the boudoir. The chandelier is Louis XV and the prie-dieu is Louis XVI. The seventeenth-century paintings of the "Four Seasons" are by Arcimboldo.

In this sunny living room, the parquet de Versailles floors, stained black and waxed, offer an interesting contrast to the walls, linen curtains, rug, and linen damask upholstered furniture, all of which are in shades of white. The low tables are Chinese, the painted desk at the far end is Louis XV, and the large gilt Louis XVI tole tree by the window is one of a pair. Color is added throughout the room by soft brown and tangerine covering the chairs. (House of Dr and Mrs. Leon Levy.)

Creating a
Twentieth-Century
Tradition

BY ANNE URQUHART
OF SMYTH, URQUHART AND MARCKWALD, INC.

MIRIAM SMYTH, ANNE URQUHART, DOROTHY MARCKWALD, AND ISABEL NOYES ARE four decorators whose work has ranged from private clients and business offices to the largest transatlantic passenger liners this country has ever built.

In 1936, the partnership evolved from the office of Elsie Cobb Wilson, who was one of the first well-known professional decorators in America. Mrs. Wilson started her practice before the First World War, which makes the firm's record of work a long and voluminous one. In fact, one of the partners is now helping the third generation of a family of clients, and part of this work is being carried out by the third generation of a family of artisans who have been associated with the office since its beginning.

The same fundamental theories which were followed in Mrs. Wilson's day have continued as the guidelines ever since, with, of course, changes in interpretation to suit the changes of the times. Some of these basic beliefs are that a decorator's responsibility is to help a client carry out the most successful possible realization of her own ideas—not to impose the decorator's "style" on her—and to try constantly to combine the best new designs and ideas with the valuable starting

OPPOSITE: The carved oak Louis XIII staircase with its terra-cotta tile treads is part of a seventeenth-century French château, Le Petit Thons, which originally stood near Dijon and was carefully dismantled and reassembled on Long Island. The bronze figure in the entrance hall is by the contemporary sculptor, Wheeler Williams. (House of Mrs. Samuel Welldon.)

points of the classic past. This injection of the present can give rooms life, freshness, and vitality, even though the background may be completely traditional.

The partners believe the first step in good decorating should be the idea, the mental picture or atmosphere of the room—or house or apartment—as a whole, aiming at beauty, and always at suitability for the people who will live in it and the purpose it will be put to. Then one should try to hold on to this fundamental idea through all the necessary compromises due to expense, time, or the necessity of using Mother-in-law's discarded furniture.

Their description of the "perfect" decorator is one with: *First:* The talent, taste, and background of knowledge and tradition needed to design beautiful rooms of many different kinds, all suitable frameworks for present-day living. *Second:* A psychological insight good enough to understand the wishes of the inarticulate client who can't describe the atmosphere she wants, and to recognize the right time to encourage some experimental idea even when faced with the "my husband wouldn't like it" defense. *Third:* The brain of a small IBM computer to be able to answer quickly that first question, "What will it cost to furnish this apartment?", to stay within a budget, and to keep one's own business solvent, while holding the creative side of the work always in first place. *Fourth:* The drive and capacity needed to pull together all the separate elements of the work and to get a job done even nearly on time.

It is a great compliment to a decorator, but still a shock, to be taken by a client into an unsatisfactory room or a newly acquired empty apartment and asked point-blank, "What would you do here?" and the fact that it happens seems to prove that the outsider sees decorating as a much simpler art than it really is. Probably only professionals with years of experience realize the tremendous variety of the work involved even when only private clients are considered; when the decorating of large ships is added, the unusual problems and experiences are compounded.

Although there is a big gap between working in a Park Avenue apartment and in a shipyard, it is not impossible to bridge, as the same faculties are required in both cases. The ability to hold on to an idea with one hand while hammering away with the other at details to achieve, for instance, the best curtains for a client's dining room, is really no different from the ability to thread one's way through the complications of checking fireproof requirements of furnishings for an entire ship without losing sight of its whole and final appearance. One of the first shocks to the partners when work was started on the S.S. *United States* was to find that a set of blueprints was too long to be unfolded in their office (unless the window was open). But that was not very different from the day sixty yards of chintz waved from the third-floor office window, with a client pulling in the upper end as the roller hit Madison Avenue, starting the runaway of one of the last horse-drawn junk carts ever seen there.

In the early days, the few professional decorators, like Elsie Cobb Wilson, were people of great knowledge and training, and of very good, disciplined taste. Now decorating has become an enormous industry with, unavoidably, many inadequately trained "practitioners," and this fact has had a noticeable and unfortunate effect on the standards of many manufacturers.

Smyth, Urquhart, and Marckwald believe that there should be an effort on the part of the professional decorators to lead the clients toward a type of interior that would be expressive of

American life—gay, unaffected, and inventive, but with a solid foundation of good design and quality and an unobtrusive sense of practicality. The clients and the public must help to encourage this atmosphere if they believe in it, as the decorators cannot do it all alone. As Manet developed his theories of painting, he said he was not a revolutionist but that he wanted to lead tradition and not follow it. In that spirit it should be possible to create a twentieth-century tradition worthy of a place in the history of decorating.

There was a fine moment in the twenties and thirties when a new style seemed to be evolving which was not a copy of the past, but not as severe as the "superoffice" style of today. At that time, many of the best European artists were interested in decorative art and, as splendid workmanship was still available and prices were not so frightening, beautiful, original, and unusual objects could be found which were really usable works of art. Matisse designed and inspired printed materials; Dufy did printed cotton panels and designs for tapestry screens and chair coverings; Dunand made his beautiful lacquer furniture and screens, not copying the Chinese but doing work of the same excellence. Miro and Lurçat designed rugs, and Redon's enchanting bunches of flowers were woven into chair seats by the Aubusson factory.

It is hoped that the present generation will find comparable objects of really fine design and good workmanship too, but this will not happen to any great extent unless people think and study and care a lot about it, and also demand good quality on every level from those who work for them. It is to the high standards set by the clients, their good taste, intelligent interest, trust, and encouragement that the best work is due; without them the greatest ideas would still exist only on paper.

The partners of Smyth, Urquhart, and Marckwald are all thoroughly convinced that decorating is one of the most interesting ways for a woman to earn her living, and they consider themselves extremely fortunate to have chosen it as a profession. Anyone with the true spirit of the decorator finds early that the lure of decorating, the interesting people one meets in connection with it, the excitement of accomplishing a good and original job, and the stimulus of hard work when it is done with congenial people all make a life and an interest that would be hard to replace. As Miriam Smyth puts it, "Once you have put your hand on the electric wire [of decorating], you can't take it off."

OPPOSITE: An elevator vestibule. In order to give a sense of space to the very small area the walls were decorated with *trompe l'oeil* paintings by Martin Battersby. The simulated scenes, pictures, and ornaments represent the interests and hobbies of the family. (Apartment of Mrs. John Jay Ide.)

OVERLEAF: Imported pine paneling from an old English house was altered to fit the living room of a bachelor's apartment. The mellow tone of the pine provides a pleasing background for the pictures, books, and antique English furniture.

Three rooms in the house of Mrs. Samuel Welldon. In the living room (above) a great deal of the interest is due to the beautiful seventeenth-century paneling brought to America when Le Petit Thons château was moved from Dijon (see also page 136). The gold, white, blue, and green of the Louis XV Savonnerie rug provided the key to the color scheme used.

The walls of the dining room are a light gray, the rug is oyster white, and the silk curtains are pale yellow, all of which subtly enhance the colors in the painting over the sideboard. The rare eighteenth-century table from the William Odom collection opens like a book and turns to seat eight people.

BELOW: In the thirty-foot-high circular tower guest room the old French wall-paper screen successfully hides a staircase leading to the courtyard below, and the unusually tall bed canopy appears to lessen the extreme height of the room. The pink-beige walls and the off-white rug set off the blues and greens of the screen.

PREVIOUS PAGE: When "Mr. Mac" retired from the English Department of the Hotchkiss School, he and his wife built a pink stucco house in the Berkshires. In the living room the bleached checkerboard birch paneling and tray ceiling make a contemporary background for traditional furniture. One of the interesting pieces is the small English elmwood lacemaker's chair near the fireplace. The changing seasons, framed by the large windows, paint a new picture every few months. (House of Mr. and Mrs. John McChesney.)

BELOW: A dining room combining French and English antiques. The paneled wall was designed to show the owner's rare collection of china. An old French wallpaper is used on the other walls and a Savonnerie rug covers the floor.

Two views of Mr. and Mrs. George Henry Warren's American Federal house in Newport, Rhode Island. A suitable background was created for the diversified interests of the owners—Mr. Warren's collection of sixteenth- and seventeenth-century rapiers and daggers and eighteenth-century gun and ship models, and Mrs. Warren's collection of contemporary works of art, including watercolors by Cézanne, Dufy, and Picasso. The unusual length of the room, which was originally the "front and back parlours" characteristic of houses of the period, dictated the furniture arrangement.

In this small salon the soft pink curtains, the Italian marble mantel, and the beige and pink design of the antique Karabagh rug make a color scheme complementary to the fine old paneling. (House of Mrs. Samuel Welldon.)

The screens in Mr. and Mrs. Irving Berlin's dining room are made of old Chinese painted leather, a wall covering used in Mrs. Berlin's father's house. They give the room originality and set the colors for the walls, rug, and curtains.

The drawing room in Mr. and Mrs. Irving Berlin's house shows how the thoughtful arrangement of many well-loved objects has made a livable and individual room within a formal, classic framework. Family portraits are given added intensity by contrast with the soft colors of the walls and furniture. The portrait of Katherine Duer Mackay, Mrs. Berlin's mother, is by Boldini.

Two rooms in the apartment of Mr. and Mrs. Augustus J. Murray.

ABOVE: In the dining room, the use of color is free and gay, combining the blue in the ground of the scenic paper with the brilliant coral velvet of the chairs. A marbleized console applied to a mirrored panel decorates one wall, the mirror making the room look wider, particularly at night, when the soft glow of lighted candles reflects in it.

RIGHT: In the living room, the panel of "*Les Monuments de Paris*" by Dufour and Leroy established the color scheme—light green-blue walls, off-white self-striped silk curtains, a beige carpet, and textured blue upholstery. A particularly interesting piece is the revolving bookstand in the corner.

A delightful combination of the past and the present in the Newport house of Mr. and Mrs. George Henry Warren. The wallpaper, designed by Marie Laurençin in the 1920s, seems perfectly at home in this room of an earlier architectual period, with the eighteenth-century porcelains and the old French chair which is covered with needlework recently made by Mrs. Warren. (The living room in the same house appear in black and white on page 149.)

A simple background serves as a foil for fine antique furniture and ornaments in the living room. Contemporary freshness and life are added by the gay twentieth-century paintings and by such touches as the soft covers, which were specially embroidered for the room. The dining room is the fourth in which Mrs. Knight Woolley has used her Adam chairs, her gold dishes and candelabra, and the fine contemporary rug made for her by Boiceau in France in 1930. The dark brown polished walls give a sense of depth and space.

A New Look at Decorating

BY MICHAEL TAYLOR

I WAS YOUNG, I WAS IN CALIFORNIA, AND IT WAS TIME, MANY OF US HERE FELT, FOR A FRESH approach to decorating. The climate of my native state, the quality of light, and the ready availability of plants, and of various types of growing things, all contributed to bringing about what has been hailed by many as a "new look" in decorating. The underlying quality of this "new look" can perhaps best be described as rooms in which a feeling of air and lightness predominates. To achieve this effect I began to use a great deal of white, which has a way of opening up a room and giving it a fresh, open-air-living quality.

When I first began this type of decorating, I was really not responsible for a "new look" so much as I was for bringing back the "white look" which Syrie Maugham had created in the America of the twenties. At that time white in all shades was frequently used almost to the exclusion of other colors in certain fashionable houses, but in the intervening three decades, with the rapid and almost frenzied prewar and postwar succession of fads, gimmicks, trends, and trick schemes, white was almost forgotten.

People have often said to me, "But you don't use much color." This is not so at all. I build a simple background—usually of white or of a very light shade—for the *use* of color. This simpli-

OPPOSITE: The first-floor powder room in the French country house of Mr. and Mrs. Louis Benoist retains the Victorian plushness of an earlier epoch. The splendid carved gilt mirror was brought by sail around the Horn. In the mahogany framed copper tub Anna Held took her famous champagne bath while visiting the Almadèn Vineyards. French cotton with colorful cabbage roses covers the walls and even upholsters the tub. The cotton rug is a matching rose-pink.

city of background gives the feeling of freshness and space and adds a certain note of purity against which the simple lines of fine furniture show to their best advantage. It also makes the one color, or the several colors used, seem more vivid and important.

Actually there is a tremendous amount of color in my rooms, but there are not *many* colors. Light, as we know, contains in itself all colors, so that from the simple background the main color I use in the room travels rapidly and with no competing wave lengths to the eye. For this reason I find I can use very little color, proportionately speaking, in my rooms, and yet achieve an effect of color and brightness. I have always felt that a good room should be predominantly of one color. On entering it one might feel that it is a white and green room, or a white and blue room, with other colors introduced for accent, but essentially it will be a white room or a green room, or a blue room with a contrasting color used in lesser proportion. For this reason I am more apt to use a pattern continually throughout a room, keeping to the same color rather than mixing patterns or prints.

Of vital importance is the problem of light—how much natural light is available in a room by day, and how the room is to be illuminated at night—both of which must influence the choice of a color scheme. At night, I like the feeling of white lamps because of the bright way colors react to them. In the daytime, rooms should of course be allowed to capture as much natural light (though not direct sunlight) as possible. When designing a room one must take note of the exposure, as certain colors react unfavorably to certain types of light. It is difficult to make rules, except in the case of white, which is seldom an unsuitable choice. Yellow is a good first color in a room with a northern exposure. In a room facing east, color must be chosen with the knowledge that there will be constant glare and change of lighting throughout the day. Therefore, in creating a fresh, airy look, careful attention must be paid to exposure as well as color, all of which is part of the theory and mechanics of light.

In addition to simple white backgrounds, correct light exposures, and the selection of a first-value color, I have another device which has become almost a trade-mark of my decorating. Whenever possible I introduce growing things into my rooms. Plants have a way of preventing a room from appearing overdecorated; they also soften the light. Cut flowers, lovely though they are, are expensive in the city, and if you live in the country it is usually quite a job keeping the house filled with fresh garden flowers—even in summertime. So from my point of view the perfect answer lies in using indoor plants. This type of decoration admittedly may be easier in California than in many areas where the climate is more inclement, yet with air-conditioning and other such improvements it is becoming more practical to grow plants indoors.

This feeling for naturalism has also influenced my attitude toward the treatment of wood. Although I like painted furniture, and use it a great deal, I prefer most woods in their natural or near-natural state. I particularly dislike furniture that has been overstained or overcolored, and I always prefer the softer, natural-finish woods to the highly polished or glazed surfaces.

OPPOSITE: In this light and airy bedroom, Michael Taylor has included not one object or one color too many. The English *chinoiserie* bed and bench in pickled pine and the trimly buttoned and bowed chairs are copies of antiques from the Syrie Maugham collection. The Venetian mirror is also a collector's item of rare beauty.

159

Antique French and Italian furniture and two brilliant yellow candlesticks from Portugal mix comfortably with modern pieces in this house at Pebble Beach, California, of Mr. and Mrs. DeWitt Rucker. The floor is a natural overscaled herringbone design in pine. Mrs. Rucker's extensive collection of blue and white Chinese export is seen in the adjoining blue and white garden room.

OPPOSITE: A paneled screen made of an old French *boiserie* provides an impressive background to the sofa and balances an ornate mantel on the opposite side of the living room. The old unpainted woods make a warm, mellow background for the cool greens and whites of the furniture and rug, adding a contrasting mood of the past to an otherwise predominantly contemporary room. (House of Mr. and Mrs. Paul Avery.)

Three rooms in the California house of Mr. and Mrs. William E. Roberts.

LEFT: Natural burlap covers the walls, bed, and pillows in the boy's bedroom. The beams and window panels are of hand-hewn wood. The furniture is early seventeenth-century Spanish and the decoy at the window is early American.

OPPOSITE: The old fireplace sets a Gothic theme for the warm and intimate dining room. Brilliant red burlap covers the walls and ceiling and is used for curtains. The rare set of early English chairs is covered in Cordovan leather. The chandelier is Mexican.

BELOW: In the adjoining boys' study, with its unusual fireplace, the French willow chairs are upholstered and covered in brilliant magenta-colored wool. The collage is by Jean Varda.

The two rooms below are in the house of Mr. and Mrs. Louis Benoist. In the sitting room, blue and white are used exclusively to set off a fine collection of blue and white Chinese export porcelain. The French chairs are upholstered in quilted white linen and bordered in blue. The enchanting white faïence stove is a Louis XVI piece. The adjoining master bedroom, which retains the feeling of the rest of the house, is covered with a very delicate blue and white flowered cotton print. The brass four-poster is an antique "marriage bed" curtained in embroidered Swiss batiste.

A room designed for the display of the owner's impressive antique gun collection. The walls of bleached pine and the planked floors lend a country flavor. The glass area in the west wall had to be limited because of the intensity of the midday sun, but the plastic skylight in the roof helps to equalize the light. The Austrian stove contains a gas heating unit. (House of Mr. and Mrs. Brooks Walker.)

ABOVE: A magnificent view across San Francisco is reflected in the mirrored walls of Mr. and Mrs. Peter Bercut's penthouse drawing room. To add further to the feeling of space, a tiny conservatory was created in one corner fenced off with glass and two mirrored walls. The furniture provides a note of traditional elegance in a modern setting.

When I am asked exactly what I am doing that is different in decorating, I find it difficult to answer, because most of the things I emphasize have been used to a greater or lesser extent by other decorators for many years. However, my approach is to combine everything suitable that gives a room the feeling of freshness, originality, and a more beautiful atmosphere for living. Every decorator must have somewhat the same approach, but differences must always lie in the personal ways in which the same or similar ideas are carried out.

When I first start to work for a client, I am particularly anxious to help him develop a feeling of complete freedom in exploring the relationships between periods, color, and room arrangements. In this age of conformity to the so-called "correct" trends, I strongly believe that people should have the satisfaction of developing their own personal tastes and of expressing themselves in their own homes with originality, and, if they so wish, with unorthodoxy. A good decorator should encourage his client to develop his own taste in whichever direction this may lie; he should try to give him more authority in his personal likes and dislikes; he should lead him to understand that there really is no law which says that we can't today choose any style, any period, or any approach. No one should be too strongly influenced or hampered by what he has seen done before, or by what he has been told should or should not be done to decorate a certain type of house or room. If one is free in one's thinking, one has so much more fun with decorating. One is more excited, *and* exciting, and the final outcome is likely to be much more rewarding. Current trends or fashions should never be allowed to inhibit or destroy a person's creativity and confidence. Fashions are there to be observed and to be considered, but they should not be allowed to dictate. A good room, designed today, should give one, on entering, the exciting feeling that the owner is a part of it and that it is for him a personal triumph, whether or not it follows a recognizable trend.

From the above it is obvious that I have no feeling at all against mixing styles and periods. In fact, I am very much in favor of it. With few exceptions I do not think that one period is more beautiful than another. Attractive designs can be found in almost any period, and certainly there is no arbitrary law which says that an eighteenth-century French chair and a Sheridan can't be used in the same room. The only consideration is how well these or other pieces look together; do they compete with each other or do they create a felicitous sense of contrast?

This last element is important. To be successful, a room must contain the element of contrast —in forms as well as in colors and textures. If a room is too rich, or if the furniture is all too ornate, or all too primitive, the room is wrong. It is contrast that brings it excitingly alive. This applies to materials too. If a room uses velvet extensively, for instance, a very crude linen, or a tapestry that seems crude compared to the velvet, should be introduced for contrast. As a result the velvet be-

Opposite:
FAR LEFT: Smoky browns with white, wood shutters instead of curtains, low sofas and chairs with plain-textured draperies invite the brilliant colors of the outdoors by day and give a protected warm feeling to the living room by night. The tops of old stone columns are imaginatively used for tables. The giant sconce between the windows is a rare Italian antique. (House of Mr. and Mrs. William E. Roberts.)

LEFT: A collection of early French, Portuguese, and Chinese export faïence provides color and charm for this all-white dining room. The French provincial chairs are covered in soft glove leather. (House of Mr. and Mrs. William Green.)

comes more beautiful, and the linen or tapestry more handsome. Very often a room featuring silk and satin and velvet is a terrible bore because the combination is too rich and creates a feeling of surfeit.

When a new house or a room has been put together and the practical needs have been attended to, and everything is in working order, how much further should a decorator go? This is a question that arises constantly. It is my conviction that a decorator can prepare only the mood of the room or house. The client must then live in it and develop a personal feeling toward it so that it becomes something that belongs to him and to no one else. Usually it takes many years to develop a really beautiful house, for it must grow with the personalities involved. Mementos, paintings, accessories—objects collected by the owners themselves are the things that make a house personal. It is very easy for a decorator to finish a room or a house too quickly, to overfinish, over-decorate, or "overaccessorize" it. My creed is simplicity, and I think this is always the most sensible approach. If a room is kept simple, and if it works well, nine times out of ten it *looks* well. Further, if it seems to belong to the house and to the owner, it has an additional reason for being and usually is a beautiful place to enter.

Everyone who has done a certain amount of decorating must have experienced the feeling that a room is attractive but is still somehow just not quite right. In this case invariably my advice is to take something out. Try it simpler, remove some of the accessories, eliminate that "added" piece of furniture that was recently brought in. A simpler room is a better room. If it is properly put together, it is often more refreshing to have a wall with nothing hanging on it. Not every corner of a room has to be decorated, not every table has to be covered or every wall filled with paintings or prints. Perhaps a valuable lesson we can learn from Europe is that one of the great charms of the best English and Continental houses is that they are not overly furnished.

This fits in with my conviction that the most beautiful rooms are those that retain a feeling of not being quite finished. There is still a place for a painting on that wall, still a chair to be found that will suit that corner . . . meanwhile the room stays alive, young and growing. Directly it is finished to a point that nothing can be added or advantageously changed, it somehow becomes static and decadent.

At the risk of sounding contradictory I would like to add that, while a room should be beautiful, it should not be "too perfect." Perfection in every detail usually makes a room look studied, formal, rather dull, and even forbidding. For a room to appear human and personal, besides not being quite finished, some small thing should remain that is not entirely according to the book—perhaps a chair placed a little off the right angle, or a lamp that has more personality than elegance.

It is possible to speak in only general terms about the things that bring a room to life, for this may vary in every case. Sometimes an owner may have a collection which is of personal interest and value but is absolutely not of the period, thinking, or mood of the room in which he would like to place it. I say, "Try it," for it may turn out to be just the thing to bring it alive, and in being bold enough to experiment you may find that you have created an original style. In the final analysis, new ideas are simply solutions to new problems.